MASTER YOUR BREATH, TRANSFORM YOUR LIFE

MASTER YOUR BREATH, TRANSFORM YOUR LIFE

UNLOCK THE HIDDEN POWER OF BREATHWORK TO HEAL, AWAKEN AND PROSPER

CHRISTOPHER AUGUST

Christopher August
Master Your Breath, Transform Your Life
Unlock The Hidden Power of Breathwork To Heal, Awaken and Prosper

Published by Spines Publishing Platform
ISBN: 979-8-89569-553-1

CONTENTS

HOW TO USE THIS BOOK

This book can be read from cover to cover like a traditional book, or you can use it as an interactive resource for your personal growth. It includes both written exercises and guided breathwork practices, which are available on the **"Beats and Breath" app**, to help you connect more deeply with your body, emotions, and energy. By engaging with these exercises and practices, you'll be able to integrate the teachings in each chapter through direct experience.

This is your personal journey of transformation, and I encourage you to approach it with curiosity, openness, and self-compassion. Some chapters or exercises may challenge you to explore deeper layers of yourself, while others may feel light and expansive. Both are essential to your growth. The more fully you engage with this process, the more profound the shifts will be.

To download the Beats and Breath app, simply go to the **"Additional Resources"** section at the back of the book and scan the QR code for either the iOS or Android app with your phone camera. Once you've downloaded the app, you can opt in for a free 7-day trial to access all the breathwork practices provided in this book.

It's important to approach these practices with care and mindfulness. Breathwork can sometimes bring up intense emotional or physical sensations, especially during deeper practices. If at any point you feel lightheaded, dizzy, or overwhelmed, stop the practice, return to normal breathing, and take time to rest. These reactions are normal, but it's essential to listen to your body and proceed at your own pace.

Please note that these practices are not intended to diagnose, treat, or cure any medical or psychological condition. They are designed for educational and personal growth purposes only. If you have a severe medical condition or are pregnant, please consult with your licensed healthcare provider or mental health professional before beginning any new breathwork routine to ensure that these practices are safe for you.

INTRODUCTION: THE INVISIBLE FORCE WITHIN

It's no secret we live in unprecedented times. The winds of change are blowing strong, and we find ourselves at a turning point in the evolution of human consciousness. We are undergoing a collective transformation, and everything we have known to be true is now being brought into question. This moment in history is more than a passing phase; it represents a seismic shift, one that will reshape the fabric of reality itself.

As our political, economic, and social structures fracture and disintegrate, we are being called to rise into a new paradigm—one rooted in connection, community, compassion, and authenticity. This emerging world values co-existence and co-creation over the archaic models of domination, control, and exploitation. But before we can truly step into this higher frequency, we must first turn inward to optimize our bodies, recalibrate our minds, and open our hearts. It's an internal revolution that requires each of us to reclaim our power and purpose.

And yet, in today's modern, fast-paced society, this journey inward can feel like an insurmountable challenge. With an unending torrent of information, thoughts, and distractions constantly bombarding our minds, and with ever-increasing demands on our time, we often feel stretched to our breaking point. The balancing act of work, relationships, family, finances, and self-care becomes so overwhelming that life itself can feel like a never-ending cycle of chaos. In this constant state of mental and emotional overload, it's easy to lose touch with our true selves, leaving us stressed, anxious, and disconnected. Burnout becomes the norm, and the distance between who we are and who we long to be grows wider.

Perhaps you, too, feel this deep shift happening, sensing that both you and the world around you are rapidly changing, and you're wondering what's next. Maybe you find yourself at a crossroads, contemplating what's next. Deep down, you know you're meant for something more, something extraordinary, but you find yourself swimming in a sea of uncertainty. At times, it can feel like your life is collapsing under the weight of a never-ending list of responsibilities and expectations. Your heart longs for meaning, fulfillment, and a deeper connection to your purpose, yet the hamster wheel keeps spinning, pulling you deeper into cycles of worry, doubt, fear, and mediocrity.

You're not alone.

Across the globe, countless individuals are grappling with similar challenges that compromise their health and well-being. According to Mental Health America, nearly 20 percent of Americans—roughly 50 million people—are experiencing some form of mental illness. Another study from Harvard Medical School estimates that, globally, one out of two people will be impacted by poor mental health or mental illness at some point in their lives. These statistics underscore the urgent need for us to explore new pathways and approaches to how we live and lead our lives.

To navigate these turbulent times, we must learn how to cultivate the inner strength, vitality, courage, and confidence necessary to break free from the limitations and blockages that hinder our highest potential. This journey of self-discovery and empowerment begins with the simplest yet most overlooked tool: our breath.

Breath is life. It is the first thing we do when we enter this world and the last thing we do before we leave it. Despite its critical role in our physiological and psychological well-being, many of us move through life unaware of the true power our breath holds. The breath is not just a mechanism for survival; it is a gateway to profound freedom and transformation. In the busyness of modern life, it's easy to underestimate the breath as a means to experience the happiness, harmony, and balance we seek. But imagine if simply becoming aware of your breath and learning to harness its potential could dramatically shift your entire life experience?

The breath serves as a conductor, catalyst, and instrument for both grounding and expansion. It is the thread that weaves together all aspects of our being, connecting the physical, mental, emotional, and spiritual realms. It is the rhythm of our soul, orchestrating the sacred and celestial dance of life within us. Our breath is a tuning fork for the spirit, aligning and harmonizing us with our higher self and true nature. It bridges the gap between the tangible and the intangible, the known and the unknown, the human and the divine. By transitioning from unconscious to conscious awareness of our breath, we open the door to transformative change.

The truth is, you don't need to add another tool or practice to experience a shift. What you need is something simple and accessible, something you already possess and can use anytime, anywhere. When you learn to breathe with intention and awareness, you unlock the ability to cultivate balance and well-being in every area of your life. In fact, ancient wisdom, modern science, and holistic healing experts all align with the idea that the quality of each breath is the single most powerful tool we have to nurture total physical, emotional, cognitive, and spiritual well-being.

Consider the challenges you're facing right now—whether it's stress at work, tension in your relationships, struggles with finances, or the general feeling of being overwhelmed by life. What if, instead of feeling like you're constantly on the verge of burnout, you could approach these challenges with a calm and clear mind? What if, instead of reacting out of frustration or fear, you could respond with grace and confidence? Your breath is the pathway to that kind of transformation.

Think about this...

Think about this: every minute, you take about 16 breaths. That's roughly 960 breaths every hour, 23,000 breaths a day, and more than 8 million breaths each year. What if just a small fraction of those breaths could be used intentionally to shift your state of mind, regulate your emotions, and unlock your highest potential? Imagine waking up each day feeling grounded, energized, and deeply connected to yourself and the world around you. Picture approaching life's challenges not with anxiety or overwhelm, but with clarity, confidence, and calm.

Your breath is not just a tool to help you manage stress or get through the day. It is a timeless technology that can help you create a life filled with unlimited possibilities and potential—a life in which you are living your dreams, feeling fully alive, and thriving in every way.

The great news is that you don't have to be a yogi or spend hours in meditation to benefit from mastering your breath. All you need is a pair of lungs and a willingness to explore the profound power within you. Trust that with each conscious breath, you are moving closer to the life you've always wanted.

This book is not just another self-help guide filled with empty promises. It is a comprehensive, practical, and heart-centered approach to transforming your life from the inside out. Drawing on ancient wisdom, modern science, and personal stories of profound transformation, this guide offers you tools, techniques, practices, and insights that you can integrate into your daily life, no matter where you are on your journey.

As you turn these pages, remember that you are the expert of your own experience. No book, system, or guru can replace the innate wisdom residing within you. If what you read resonates, embrace it fully. If it doesn't, move on and explore what feels true to your path. All that is required is an open mind, a willing heart, and a commitment to your breath.

I invite you to take a moment right now. Pause. Close your eyes and take a deep, intentional breath. Feel the air fill your lungs, expanding your chest and belly. Hold it for a moment, then exhale slowly, letting go of any tension or stress you're holding onto. That breath you just took—it's not just a breath; it's an invitation to step into a new way of being.

If you're ready to explore the incredible power within you, to breathe deeply into the life you've always dreamed of, then let us begin this journey together. With each conscious breath, you will move closer to a life of true liberation.

FROM THE EDGE OF DEATH TO THE POWER OF BREATH

There are moments in life when everything changes. Moments so profound they etch themselves into your soul and lift the veil between the seen and unseen to reveal truths that were always there but hidden in plain sight. These defining times call into question everything we knew to be true and ask us to leave our comfort zone and embark on a journey into the unknown. For many, this call manifests in the form of a life crisis or challenge, or a catalyst such as the loss of a job, a relationship challenge, a health problem, an accident, a financial setback, or the death of a loved one. For others, it may show up as divine intervention, synchronicity, or a soul calling to leave their current situation and start anew.

For me, this moment came in the heart of Africa where I was faced with a sudden near-death experience. In this moment I encountered the breath not as a mere function, but as a lifeline, a whisper of grace that held me between the worlds of life and death. It was there, in the rapids of the Zambezi River, that ultimately led me to discover who I am and why I'm here.

But before we traverse this path further, let's travel back in time to where it all started.

I grew up the suburbs of Buffalo, NY, living life in a lower-middle class home. Although my home life was less than stable (emotionally and financially speaking), I had two parents who cared for and loved me, but not so much each other. As a highly sensitive and intuitive young boy I unconsciously absorbed everything in my environment, causing me to experience an internalized form of anxiety. However, that didn't stop me from enjoying my childhood. Those early days revolved around sports - playing sports, trading sports cards and watching sports with my neighborhood friends. Each week after school and during the summers we got together to play football, hockey, basketball, baseball or frisbee, or a variation of them all. I didn't care much for school, except gym class. I often found myself drifting in a haze of boredom, counting the minutes until I could return to the company of my friends.

As I transitioned from childhood into my pre-teens, my interests expanded from sports to girls, but the underlying theme of escape remained constant. At the age of ten, I was thrust into my first major trauma: my parents' divorce. The months leading up to that moment were filled with heightened tension and relentless arguments. The sense of impending doom only magnified my anxiety. I vividly remember the night it happened—I locked myself in my room for two days, vowing never to emerge.

Over the next year, things spiraled further. Our home was repossessed due to non-payment, forcing my mother, sister, and me to relocate. Thankfully, my grandfather, my greatest mentor, intervened, purchasing a house a few blocks away. With my father gone, my mother had to work two jobs to make ends meet. It was an intense time for all of us, and as I entered my teenage years, I took on the role of the "man" of the house, shouldering the weight of the responsibility that came with it. I worked at my uncle's restaurant, sweeping floors and washing dishes, while also working other odd jobs, often handing over my earnings to my mother for groceries and bills. At school, my academic performance was lackluster at best; I barely scraped by, failing most classes except for a few. Life felt like an endless uphill battle. At fourteen, I began drinking alcohol and smoking weed with friends as a means of escaping the ever-present fear and worry that lived within me.

As spring of my senior year in high school approached, my future was clouded in uncertainty. I had no scholarships, no college offers, and no clear direction. I enrolled in a community college nearby while working at a Lexus dealership detailing cars. After two years, I was accepted into the University at Buffalo, where I earned a bachelor's degree in communication. At the time, I believed that adhering to the societal blueprint for success—attending school and securing a corporate job—would bring me happiness. Following graduation, I secured a position as a Market Development Specialist at a global tech firm while pursuing my master's degree in Organizational Leadership by night. By 2012, I completed my M.A., graduating at the top of my class. At work, I was being groomed by the vice president to climb the corporate ladder. To the outside world, it seemed like I had it all—a downtown apartment, a new car, and quarterly vacations. Yet, beneath this façade, I felt lost and hollow. I realized I had sacrificed my own dreams to build someone else's, leading a life devoid of meaning and purpose. I desperately yearned for something more—a life beyond the confines of a desk, a life where I could make a tangible difference. I prayed for signs to guide me on this quest, and eventually, a beacon appeared.

FROM THE BOARDROOM TO THE VILLAGES OF AFRICA

I remember it vividly. As I drove home from work one evening, a billboard caught my eye. In bold, striking letters, it read: "Are you ready to answer the call?" At the bottom right-hand corner, it said, "Sponsored by the Peace Corps." I rushed home and delved into research on the Peace Corps—a grassroots organization funded by the U.S. government that sends volunteers to various parts of the world for two-year stints in fields like agriculture, health, business, and teaching English. It resonated deeply with me and aligned perfectly with my core values. That night, I submitted an application, and weeks later, I was invited to continue the process.

Months of rigorous physical, mental, and emotional assessments followed. Eight months later, an email arrived in my inbox:

Dear Christopher,
You have been officially accepted into the Peace Corps Tanzania as a
Health and Business Volunteer. You have seven business days to give
us your decision.

Fear surged within me, and my stomach fluttered with butterflies. Part of me wanted to retreat into the safety of the familiar, while another part—my higher self—recognized this as the opportunity of a lifetime. I knew that embarking on this journey would forever alter my life, and oh, how right I was.

In January 2014, I had a one-way ticket and found myself boarding a Boeing 767 with thirty-five other Americans bound for Tanzania—over 8,000 miles from home. We arrived exhausted and jet-lagged after an 18-hour journey. The days that followed were filled with security briefings by Peace Corps staff as they led us from the port city of Dar es Salaam to Tanga. There, we spent three months living with host families and learning Swahili, the unifying language of Tanzania. This immersion not only connected us with the local culture, it forged bonds with fellow volunteers.

Upon arriving at my host family's home, I was greeted by four children who eagerly carried my suitcases and led me into their home. We passed through a doorway—a thin blanket adorned with the colors of the Tanzanian flag—into a modest brick hut. To the right, an antiquated wooden table and couch awaited. To the left, four single mattresses lay side by side in a 12x12 room. Ahead, clay stairs descended to a courtyard where three men and three women sat around a fire, laughing and sharing stories. As I approached, their gaze shifted, locking onto me. One by one, they embraced me, their smiles warm and welcoming.

"Karibu! Habari yako?" (Welcome! How are you?) they said with big smiles. After an awkward, uncomfortable exchange in my broken Swahili, my host dad proceeded to guide me to the room where I would stay—a space with a single bed and a small wooden desk lit by candles and a kerosene lantern. Adjacent was the "bathroom"—a hole in the ground surrounded by porcelain tiles. There was no electricity, no modern conveniences, and no running water. All water had to be fetched from a village well a quarter-mile away.

I stood there, stunned. A cascade of thoughts flooded my mind: What have I gotten myself into? Did I make the right choice? Should I just go home? Despite the discomfort, I knew I had to stay and embrace this experience. Every day was an adventure, immersing me in the rhythms of village life and deepening my gratitude for the simple luxuries I had once taken for granted. The work I had deemed "real"—behind a desk and attending meetings—paled in comparison to the profound reality I was now living.

Each morning began at 5:00 a.m. with the crowing of roosters. I fetched water from the tank and lit a fire to heat water for my bucket bath. By sunrise at 6:30 a.m., the village was in full force, alive with music playing from speakers and the sweet aroma of chapati bread filling the air. After eating a traditional Tanzanian breakfast of eggs, bread, and chai tea, I headed to class to learn Swahili and specific skills to support me in my upcoming work. Those three months offered me many valuable lessons, most importantly, resilience and strength, which were the exact things I would need to survive as a volunteer over the next 24 months.

Leaving my host family was heart-wrenching. They were my first glimpse into Tanzanian life and pivotal in my journey of healing and self-discovery. After those intense three months, I embarked on a 17-hour bus ride to Songea, in the southern grasslands, just 90 km from the Mozambique border. There, in the village of Subira, I would spend the next two years.

By day, I worked as a health and business volunteer—teaching at a primary school, installing solar panels and rainwater tanks, and helping local women establish a village eatery to utilize leftover crops for the community. On my days off, I rode my mountain bike through dirt paths, exploring nearby villages. Meals were cooked over a wood fire or charcoal stove, and my clothes were washed by hand. The yearning for modern conveniences faded, replaced by a profound connection to my primal roots. Despite the challenges—physical, mental, and emotional—each moment of exhaustion became a powerful teacher, cultivating a deep sense of gratitude and appreciation.

By night, I journeyed inward, seeking answers to questions like, "Who am I? Why am I here? What is my purpose?" I read classic literature by Ernest Hemingway, Khalil Gibran, Paulo Coelho, and Henry David Thoreau. I journaled by candlelight, delving into my fears, dreams, and aspirations. I embraced yoga, meditation, and other spiritual practices to heal and expand my inner wisdom. Layer by layer, breath by breath, I uncovered both my shadow and my light—and everything in between. At times, the process was painful, and at others, blissful. Little did I know, my greatest challenge was yet to come. As I delved deeper into the Tanzanian way of life and my own inner landscapes, the true test of my resilience and growth awaited—a trial that would push the limits of my endurance and faith.

A BRUSH WITH DEATH

In December of 2014, nearly a year into my service, I embarked on a 10-day adventure from my village to Zambia, Africa, to celebrate the New Year at a music festival. But what was meant to be a thrilling escape turned into one of the most harrowing and transformative experiences of my life.

One day, I decided to venture into the heart of the Zambezi River for a white-water rafting expedition. Little did I realize then that the river was infamous for its treacherous rapids. The Zambezi, with its ferocious class five rapids, presented an awe-inspiring and intimidating challenge. As we pushed off from the riverbank, a chilling warning echoed in my mind: a girl had tragically lost her life on these very waters just a few years earlier. As we approached the first of twenty-six rapids, adrenaline surged through my veins and a sense of unease washed over me.

I was positioned at the front left of the raft, paddle in hand, feeling a mix of exhilaration and dread as the boat charged forward. The river's wild currents moved around us, and my anxiety grew as we neared the infamous section of the rapids. As the raft plunged into the first class-five rapid of the day, I was abruptly thrown from the raft, engulfed by the roaring, merciless grip of the river's powerful current.

As I was tossed and tumbled beneath the waves, disoriented and helpless, I felt panic rising within me. The river was relentless, pulling me deeper, spinning me in a vortex of chaos. I fought to surface, but the force of the water was too great. My lungs burned as I struggled for air, each moment more desperate than the last. As the world around me faded to a blur, I was consumed by a singular, primal need: to breathe.

But the river offered no mercy. I was running out of oxygen, my body growing weaker with each passing second. A cold, terrifying realization began to settle in—this could be the end. In those moments, suspended between life and death, I was acutely aware of the fragility of my existence. My thoughts became a silent plea, a fervent wish for just one more breath.

Then, as if by a miracle, a hand reached out through the chaos. A kayaker had spotted me, and with incredible speed, he pulled me from the water, saving my life. As I gasped for air, my body began to shake, coughing up water from my lungs. As my vision returned, I gazed at the bright blue sky in complete awe that I was alive. I felt an overwhelming surge of gratitude move through me. The breath that filled my lungs was the sweetest I had ever known. In that moment, I vowed never again to take it for granted.

LIVING A BREATH-CENTERED LIFE

In the aftermath of this near-death experience, I found myself in a state of deep reflection. The brush with death not only rocked the very core of who I am; it ignited a profound quest within me to find meaning. It was a wake-up call that shattered my old perceptions and illuminated the profound value of each breath. As I waded through the remnants of my previous beliefs, I grappled with existential questions: What is the essence of existence? Why am I here? It was amidst this period of introspection that the breath—an element so fundamental, yet so overlooked—began calling me.

In the months that followed, a newfound sense of clarity and purpose came over me. My initial encounter with breathwork was nothing short of serendipitous. I discovered the practice through a Kundalini yoga video given to me by another Peace Corps Volunteer. Through Kundalini, I learned how to harness the breath, using it as a tool to awaken my energy, calm my mind, and transform my consciousness. The practices I discovered in Kundalini yoga were unlike anything I had experienced before. The breathwork techniques were powerful, sometimes intense, yet deeply healing. I began to feel a profound shift within myself, as though I were being rewired from the inside out. The breath became my teacher, my guide, showing me how to tap into a wellspring of inner strength and peace that I had never known existed. However, this journey didn't stop with "Kundalini Yoga."

Driven by a newfound passion, I immersed myself in the study of various breathing modalities and certifications, each one offering unique insights into the transformative power of the breath. In the years that followed, I began to research, study, and practice various forms of breathwork, from pranayama to holotropic to rebirthing and beyond. Each modality deepened my understanding and expanded my ability to use the breath as a tool for healing and personal growth.

As I traveled my inner landscapes and ventured deeper into the practice of breathwork, I began to witness remarkable changes in my life. Physically, I felt more vital and alive; mentally, clarity emerged from the fog of confusion; emotionally, a serene steadiness replaced tumultuous waves; spiritually, a deeper awareness blossomed. These moments of insight helped me understand how deeply "breath" is intertwined with the tapestry of my existence. Breath is not just a cycle of life, it's a sacred rite of renewal, guiding me back to my truest self.

Since then, I have dedicated my life to mastering the art of breath and sharing its transformative power with others. I have traveled the world, trained in various breathwork modalities, co-founded Beats and Breath, and co-created Sonic Breathwork™, a unique practice (which you'll experience in the following chapters) that combines ancient breathing techniques with cutting-edge musical compositions and the latest advancements in bioacoustics to help people heal, awaken, and prosper in every aspect of life. Each year, our events, experiences, and mobile app continue to impact thousands of people around the globe.

While this path has been fraught with challenges and struggles, it has been the most rewarding journey of my life. Breathwork has become a personal practice as well as a beacon of inspiration and a vehicle for global healing. As I share this book with you, my mission is clear: to unlock and activate within you the awareness of breath's transformative power so you can experience freedom from the inside out. In a world that often rushes past the moment, may this knowledge serve as a crucial reminder of our profound connection to life's most essential rhythm. As you embark on your journey through these pages, I invite you to breathe deeply with an open mind and a receptive heart. Reflect on your own relationship with breath, and let it guide you toward discovering the profound magic within.

AWAKENING THE POWER WITHIN YOU

From the moment we are born, we are inundated with expectations. We are told who to be, what to do, and how to live. The blueprint for happiness and success is handed to us early: go to school, get a good job, find a partner, start a family, and retire. This script is not just suggested—it's ingrained in us. As a result, we live by the unspoken rules that tell us to keep quiet, not to rock the boat, and to follow the path laid out before us. We learn to measure our worth by our achievements and our ability to conform to societal norms. Over time, we become experts at wearing masks—hiding our true selves behind layers of roles, responsibilities, and expectations. We strive, we hustle, we perform. But in the quiet moments, when the noise fades and we are left alone with our thoughts, a quiet truth often whispers, "This isn't who I am."

Have you ever felt it? The sense that, despite all your accomplishments, something essential is missing? Maybe you've checked all the boxes, hit all the milestones, yet you feel disconnected, unfulfilled, or even lost. Perhaps you're constantly chasing the next goal, the next promotion, or the next validation, hoping it will finally fill the void inside. But no matter how much you achieve, it never feels like enough. There is always another mountain to climb, another standard to meet. In this relentless pursuit, we often lose sight of who we really are. We forget the dreams that once ignited our spirit, the passions that made us feel alive, and the truth that lies buried beneath all the "shoulds" we've accumulated over the years.

It's exhausting, isn't it? Living a life that feels more like a performance than an authentic expression of who you are. Day after day, we put on our masks, play our parts, and do what is expected. We contort ourselves to fit into molds that were never meant for us. And in the process, we become strangers to our own souls. We lose touch with our intuition, our desires, and our sense of purpose. The gap between who we are and who we pretend to be grows wider, leaving us feeling trapped in a cycle of dissatisfaction and self-doubt.

Many of us try to numb this discomfort, filling the emptiness with distractions—busy schedules, social media, shopping, substances, sex, or toxic relationships. We scroll mindlessly through our phones, binge-watch TV shows, or bury ourselves in work, anything to avoid facing the quiet voice inside that says, "There's more to life than this." But these distractions only offer temporary relief. The emptiness always returns, deeper and more insistent, reminding us that we are not living our truth.

Chances are, right now, there is a powerful urge to reset your course, recalibrate your circumstances, and chart a new trajectory; you sense a whisper from the depths of your being, calling you to step beyond the familiar confines of ordinary life and into the vast, uncharted territory of your inner world. Regardless of where you're at, you're tired of feeling like a cog in the machine and you know there's more to life than what you've been told. More than anything, you yearn to follow your passions, live authentically, and reconnect with the dreams that have been buried beneath the surface. You might not have all the answers, and you don't need to—what matters is that you've heard the call. It's a call to slow down, to strip away the noise, and to reconnect with the essence of who you are beneath all the roles you've been told to play.

If this resonates with you, you're in the right place. Something led you here—to this book, to this moment, to these words.

FROM "FALSE SELF" TO "TRUE SELF"

In the labyrinth of our inner world, the journey from the false self to the true self is nothing short of an alchemical transformation. Along the way, there are countless deaths and rebirths. As we navigate through the caverns of our inner landscape, we slowly peel back the layers of illusion to reveal the radiant core of our true essence. This transition is not just a shift in perspective; it is a profound metamorphosis that demands the shedding of illusions and the embrace of authenticity.

The false self, or ego, is often characterized by fears, insecurities, and conditioned beliefs that bind us to limitations and self-deception. It clings to comfort zones, perpetuates familiar yet unfulfilling patterns, and relies on external validation to define its worth. In contrast, the true self—our soul—is wise, unconditionally loving, creative, whole, and eternally connected to all things. It aligns with our deepest power, purpose, and potential. As you expand your consciousness, you begin to move beyond the façade of the false self, stripping away its layers and connecting with a more profound sense of being—one that is free from the constraints of ego.

Living from your true self means making choices that reflect your soul's desires rather than societal expectations. This shift brings heightened intuition, deeper empathy, and a sense of oneness with all that is. You start to trust your inner voice, recognizing it as the authentic guidance that leads you toward your highest path.

The journey you are about to embark on has no fixed destination; it's a pilgrimage of the soul, an unfolding of your most authentic self. This path is not straight or predictable, but rather a winding road filled with unexpected turns, profound realizations, and moments of both light and shadow. It is an invitation to peel back layers of illusion, confront your deepest truths, and remember who you are beneath all the roles you've been told to play and the identities you've assumed.

This journey is about dissolving the facades, reclaiming your power, and, most importantly, tapping into the pulse of your own being. The first step in this reclamation is to reconnect with the most primal aspect of your existence: your breath.

Notice the air as it enters your nostrils, cool and refreshing, and feel it as it leaves, warm and soothing. Your breath is your anchor—it's always with you, a constant companion, a bridge between your outer world and your inner landscape.

Inhale deeply through your nose, filling your lungs and allowing your belly to rise. Hold it for a moment. Now exhale slowly out of your mouth, releasing any tension, any stagnant energy, any weight you've been carrying. Feel the ground beneath you, supporting you and holding you up.

In this moment, you are not your past mistakes or your future anxieties. You are here, now, with each breath reminding you that you are enough, just as you are. "Presence is your power."

Continue this same cycle of breath ten more times.

As you come to completion, tune into the sensations in your body. What do you feel? Simply observe and notice what's arising within you. Perhaps you feel some tingling or energy moving through your body. Maybe you feel slightly clearer, lighter, and more relaxed than just a few minutes before you began.

We can do this very simple exercise throughout the day to come back into homeostasis and find our center when we feel ungrounded. But this is just the beginning of your journey back to yourself. As you continue reading, you will discover the transformative power of breathwork—tools that go far beyond calming the mind. These simple exercises will help you release old patterns, reconnect with your inner wisdom, and awaken parts of yourself you've long forgotten. With each breath, you step into a new chapter of your life, one where you are the author of your own story.

THE ORIGINS AND EVOLUTION OF BREATHWORK

Breathwork is more than just a wellness fad or trend—it is a transformative journey that spans centuries, rooted in ancient wisdom and reimagined in modern times. To truly appreciate its impact, we must first trace the threads of breathwork back to its origins and explore the diverse techniques that have emerged across cultures and eras.

At its core, breathwork can be defined as an active form of meditation that involves consciously and intentionally working with your breath to increase self-awareness and improve physical, mental, emotional, and spiritual well-being. It's one of the fastest-growing wellness modalities for good reason: it's both simple and profoundly effective in catalyzing personal transformation, inside and out.

Together, we'll explore how this ancient practice has been shaped by wisdom traditions across the globe and adapted into modern techniques that continue to change lives today. We'll also introduce some of the most influential breathwork pioneers of the modern era —individuals who have rediscovered, refined, and popularized these practices for a new generation seeking healing, wholeness, and connection.

THE WISDOM OF THE ANCIENTS

Breath, the invisible thread binding life across cultures and epochs, has always held profound significance. Long before the advent of modern science, ancient civilizations revered breath as a force that transcended the mere act of inhalation and exhalation, connecting us to the very essence of existence.

In ancient Greece, philosophers like Plato and Hippocrates recognized breath as a cornerstone of health and healing, observing that breath patterns could dramatically influence both physical and mental states. They understood that the way one breathes can alter the body's internal landscape, affecting emotions, thoughts, and overall well-being. The breath was not merely air; it was seen as a conduit to the soul, influencing the mind's clarity and the body's balance.

The ancient Egyptians believed in the "Ka," the breath of the soul—a divine gift bridging the human with the eternal. They saw breath as a vital life force that animated the body and connected it to the spiritual realm. Their practices often involved deep, rhythmic breathing during meditation and ritual, designed to maintain harmony between the earthly and the divine.

In the Hawaiian Islands, the word "Ha" symbolized the breath of life, a sacred force connecting individuals to the spirit of Aloha—the breath of love, compassion, and connection. This understanding of breath extended into their daily practices and rituals, reminding them of the interconnectedness of all life and the importance of living in harmony with nature and each other.

Across the vast expanse of the Vedic tradition, breath, or prana, is considered the vital life force permeating all living beings. The ancient yogis of India developed a sophisticated understanding of breath as the fundamental link between the body, mind, and spirit. "Pranayama," the practice of breath control, became a cornerstone of yogic disciplines designed to cleanse the mind, purify the body, and elevate the soul. The word pranayama itself combines "prana" (life force) and "ayama" (control or extension), reflecting the practice's intention to expand one's life force through conscious breathing.

Yogic masters believed that through pranayama, practitioners could gain mastery over their minds, emotions, and energy, achieving states of deep meditation and spiritual insight. Techniques like Nadi Shodhana (alternate nostril breathing) were used to balance the body's energy channels, while Kapalabhati (breath of fire) and "Bhastrika" (bellows breath) were designed to cleanse the lungs, invigorate the nervous system, and awaken inner vitality. Breath was viewed as the gateway to higher consciousness, capable of unlocking dormant potentials and transforming the practitioner on every level.

In Taoist philosophy, breathwork was integral to internal alchemy practices, where controlled breathing techniques were used to harmonize Qi, the vital energy flowing through the body. Taoist sages believed that breath was the bridge between the physical and spiritual realms, and that by cultivating breath through exercises like Qigong and Tai Chi, one could achieve longevity, mental clarity, and spiritual enlightenment.

Indigenous cultures worldwide have long used breath in rituals and ceremonies to invoke spiritual forces, communicate with ancestors, and restore communal balance. From the rhythmic breathing of Native American sweat lodge ceremonies to the deep breaths taken before chanting and singing in African and Australian rituals, breath is seen as a powerful tool for connecting with the unseen world. These practices often incorporated elemental interactions with fire, water, earth, and air, recognizing breath's profound ability to cleanse, heal, and empower.

BREATHWORK IN THE MODERN WORLD

As we move into the modern era, breathwork has experienced a resurgence, adapting to fit the evolving needs of contemporary society. This ancient wisdom has been revived and reinterpreted, blending traditional practices with scientific advancements to create accessible techniques that resonate with today's seekers.

Transpersonal psychologist Stanislav Grof was one of the key figures who brought breathwork into the modern wellness landscape. Initially exploring the human psyche through psychedelic substances, Grof's research shifted focus with the criminalization of LSD in the 1960s, leading him to develop "Holotropic Breathwork," a powerful technique that induces altered states of consciousness similar to those achieved through psychedelics but using only the breath. Holotropic Breathwork has since become a cornerstone of modern breathwork practices, offering profound insights, emotional release, and deep connection with oneself and the universe.

Leonard Orr, another pioneer, discovered the transformative potential of breath during personal experiments, which led him to develop "Rebirthing Breathwork." Orr's work focused on accessing repressed memories, often tied to the trauma of birth, to facilitate emotional release and personal transformation. His approach emphasizes conscious connected breathing—a circular breathing pattern that fosters uninterrupted flow and opens the door to psychological and spiritual breakthroughs.

A central concept in Leonard Orr's work is the idea of birth trauma, the notion that the experience of being born is a significant and often traumatic event that imprints on the psyche. According to Orr, these early imprints can lead to unconscious limiting beliefs and patterns that influence a person's entire life. "Rebirthing Breathwork" aims to access and release these imprints, allowing for greater freedom and self-awareness. Another significant aspect of Orr's teachings is the emphasis on personal responsibility and the power of thought. He believed that thoughts and beliefs shape reality, and by changing one's thinking and breathing patterns, a person could transform their life. This philosophy is closely tied to the broader movement of New Thought, which Orr was influenced by and contributed to.

Since then, numerous breathwork modalities have emerged, each with unique techniques and philosophies that cater to a wide range of needs and intentions. Practices such as Transformational Breath, Shamanic Breathwork, the Buteyko Method, the Wim Hof Method,

Soma Breath and our signature breathwork practice at Beats and Breath, Sonic Breathwork™ all offer distinct approaches to healing, self-exploration, and personal growth.

TYPES OF BREATHING

Breathing techniques can be broadly categorized into sympathetic and parasympathetic practices, much like the nervous system itself. Sympathetic breathing techniques, characterized by rapid or forceful breaths, stimulate alertness and energy, often inducing altered states of consciousness. In contrast, parasympathetic techniques involve slow, deep breathing to promote relaxation and recovery.

Sympathetic Breathing Techniques

- **Kapalabhati (Breath of Fire):** A dynamic practice from Kundalini Yoga that involves rapid, forceful exhales through the nose followed by passive inhales. It stimulates energy, clears the mind, and invigorates the digestive system.
- **Holotropic Breathing**: Involves continuous, rapid breathing, often through the mouth. This technique facilitates entry into non-ordinary states of consciousness, revealing profound insights and emotional release.
- **Conscious-Connected Breathing**: A circular breathing pattern with no pauses between inhalation and exhalation. It fosters an uninterrupted flow of breath, often leading to deep emotional and psychological breakthroughs.

Parasympathetic Breathing Techniques

- **Diaphragmatic Breathing:** Also known as "belly breathing," this involves deep, slow breaths using the diaphragm. It activates the parasympathetic nervous system, reducing stress and enhancing oxygenation.
- **Nadi Shodhana (Alternate Nostril Breathing):** Involves alternating breaths through each nostril. This practice balances the flow of energy in the body, calms the mind, and alleviates stress.
- **The Microcosmic Breath:** Rooted in Taoist internal alchemy, this technique circulates and harmonizes energy (Qi) throughout the body, enhancing overall well-being.
- **Box Breathing:** Involves inhaling, holding, exhaling, and holding the breath again, each for the same count. This technique regulates the nervous system and reduces stress.
- **4-7-8 Breathing:** Involves inhaling for a count of 4, holding for 7, and exhaling for 8. It promotes relaxation and reduces anxiety.

These techniques represent just a fraction of the many breathing practices available. Each offers distinct approaches and benefits, and individual experiences may vary. To explore these techniques further, access the "Beats and Breath" app, which includes a comprehensive library of breathwork sessions and journeys.

THE BENEFITS OF BREATHWORK

Breathwork has been embraced across cultures and traditions for its profound healing potential. Today, it is utilized in various settings, from alternative therapies to corporate wellness programs and conventional healthcare.

Some of the many benefits one can experience through breathwork include:

- **Stress and Anxiety Reduction:** Breathwork lowers cortisol levels and activates the parasympathetic nervous system, fostering relaxation and reducing anxiety.
- **Improved Physical Health:** Breathwork can enhance vitality, boost immunity, aid digestion, detoxify the body, and reduce inflammation.
- **Enhanced Mood:** By increasing oxygen and blood flow to the brain, breathwork influences neurotransmitters like serotonin and dopamine, improving mood, appetite, and sleep.
- **Increased Focus, Clarity, and Creativity:** Breathwork facilitates a deep state of presence and awareness, enhancing cognitive functions.
- **Trauma Healing and Emotional Regulation:** Breathwork helps release emotional blockages and past traumas, promoting resilience and emotional well-being.
- **Spiritual Connection:** Breathwork can facilitate spiritual experiences, deepen intuition, and connect individuals to a greater sense of purpose and meaning.

Next, we will dive into the science of breathing and how the breath affects us on a physiological and psychological level.

THE MIND-BODY-BREATH CONNECTION

Our breath is not just a background process; it is the bridge that connects the mind, body, and spirit. This connection is not just a poetic metaphor—it is a profound biological reality. Each breath you take carries a hidden potential to influence your mood, your health, and even your genetic expression. But to unlock this power, you must first understand the intricate dance between your breath, your body, and your mind.

Imagine if you had a remote control for your body, a simple button you could press to calm your mind, energize your body, or reset your mood. That remote control exists, and it's called your breath. The breath is unique among bodily functions because it is both automatic and under your conscious control. You don't have to think about breathing—it happens on its own—but at any moment, you can choose to take a deep breath, hold it, or change its rhythm. This dual nature makes the breath a powerful tool for influencing your physiological and psychological states.

At its core, breathing is a complex yet beautifully orchestrated process that involves the lungs, diaphragm, brain, and nervous system. Every breath you take sends signals to your brain and body, influencing everything from your heart rate to your emotional state. The rhythm of your breath acts like a secret code, communicating directly with your nervous system and triggering specific responses. By consciously changing your breath, you can activate your body's natural ability to heal, calm, and energize.

THE AUTONOMIC NERVOUS SYSTEM: BREATH AS THE KEY TO BALANCE

Your autonomic nervous system (ANS) controls the functions of your body that occur without conscious effort, such as heartbeat, digestion, and immune response. The ANS has two main branches: the sympathetic nervous system (SNS) and the parasympathetic nervous system (PNS). These two systems work together to maintain balance, but they often pull in opposite directions.

- **The Sympathetic Nervous System (SNS):** Often referred to as the "fight or flight" response, the SNS prepares your body for action when it perceives a threat. It speeds up your heart rate, increases blood pressure, and floods your body with stress hormones like adrenaline and cortisol. This response is essential for survival in moments of danger, but in today's fast-paced world, many of us find ourselves stuck in this mode, constantly reacting to stressors that aren't life-threatening—like work deadlines, traffic jams, or the latest news headline.
- **The Parasympathetic Nervous System (PNS):** Known as the "rest and digest" response, the PNS does the opposite of the SNS. It promotes relaxation, reduces heart rate, and supports digestion and recovery. This system helps your body restore and heal, but it often gets overshadowed by the constant activation of the SNS in our daily lives.

The balance between these two systems is crucial for your overall health and well-being. Chronic activation of the SNS without adequate PNS response can lead to a range of health issues, including anxiety, depression, digestive problems, and weakened immune function. This is where your breath comes in.

THE POWER OF BREATH TO REGULATE YOUR NERVOUS SYSTEM

Conscious breathing is one of the most effective ways to influence your autonomic nervous system and bring your body back into balance. When you take slow, deep breaths, you activate the parasympathetic nervous system, signaling to your body that it's safe to relax. This can reduce stress hormones, lower your heart rate, and create a sense of calm and well-being.

Scientific Insights: Research supports this connection between breath and the ANS. A study published in *Frontiers in Psychology* (2017) found that slow-paced breathing (around six breaths per minute) enhances heart rate variability (HRV), a key marker of parasympathetic nervous system activity. HRV is associated with improved emotional regulation and resilience to stress. Another study published in The Journal of Clinical Psychiatry* (2020) explored the impact of controlled breathing on mental health. It demonstrated that slow breathing techniques could significantly reduce anxiety symptoms by enhancing parasympathetic activity and reducing sympathetic dominance.

OXYGEN AND CARBON DIOXIDE: THE BREATH'S DANCE OF LIFE

Every breath you take brings oxygen into your body and expels carbon dioxide (CO_2). While oxygen is essential for survival, carbon dioxide plays an equally important role in maintaining balance within the body. When we think of breathing, we often focus solely on oxygen intake, but CO_2 is a critical player in the physiological processes that keep us healthy.

- **Oxygen's Role:** Oxygen fuels cellular respiration, the process that produces energy in every cell of your body. Without sufficient oxygen, your cells cannot perform optimally, leading to fatigue, brain fog, and reduced physical performance.

- **Carbon Dioxide's Role:** CO_2 is not just a waste product; it helps regulate blood pH, dilate blood vessels, and facilitate the release of oxygen from hemoglobin to your tissues—a phenomenon known as the Bohr effect. Proper CO_2 levels are essential for maintaining homeostasis, and disruptions in CO_2 balance can lead to anxiety, shallow breathing, and other health issues.

THE INTERPLAY BETWEEN OXYGEN AND CO_2

The relationship between oxygen and CO_2 is intricate and vital for maintaining homeostasis. Efficient breathing ensures a balance between these gases, supporting optimal physiological function. Breathing techniques that emphasize slow, deep breaths can enhance oxygen intake and promote effective CO_2 expulsion, contributing to overall health.

James Nestor, in Breath, highlights that many modern breathing practices and lifestyles disrupt this balance, leading to shallow breathing and improper CO_2 management. This imbalance can contribute to various health issues, including anxiety, fatigue, and impaired cognitive function.

Scientific Insights: Research has demonstrated that optimal oxygenation can enhance cognitive function, physical performance, and overall health. A study published in The American Journal of Physiology* (2019) explored how oxygen availability impacts brain function. The research found that improved oxygenation could enhance cognitive performance and mental clarity, emphasizing the importance of adequate oxygen levels for brain health. Another study in the *Journal of Applied Physiology* (2021) investigated the effects of oxygen supplementation on physical performance. The findings revealed that enhanced oxygen delivery improved exercise performance and recovery, highlighting the critical role of oxygen in physical endurance and recovery.

Research underscores the importance of CO_2 in maintaining respiratory and metabolic balance. A study in *Respiratory Physiology & Neurobiology* (2020) explored the role of CO_2 in respiratory control and found that CO_2 levels significantly influence breathing patterns and overall respiratory function. Another study published in Journal of Applied Physiology* (2018) investigated the effects of CO_2 on oxygen release from hemoglobin. The research demonstrated that increased CO_2 levels facilitated greater oxygen release, highlighting the importance of CO_2 in optimizing oxygen delivery to tissues.

THE VAGUS NERVE

One of the key physiological mechanisms underlying the effects of breathwork is the activation of the vagus nerve. The vagus nerve, the longest cranial nerve, plays a crucial role in linking the brain to various organs, including the heart, lungs, and digestive tract. It is integral to the parasympathetic nervous system, which helps to calm and restore the body after stress. Nestor highlights that deep, mindful breathing enhances vagal activity, promoting relaxation and emotional stability. The vagus nerve's activation through breath has been linked to reductions in anxiety and depression, as it helps regulate mood and stress responses.

Scientific Insights: A study in *Psychiatry Research: Neuroimaging* (2018) investigated the effects of slow breathing on vagal tone and brain function. The results indicated that controlled breathing practices could increase vagal tone, leading to enhanced emotional regulation and decreased stress levels. A study in the *Journal of Clinical Psychiatry* demonstrated that vagus nerve stimulation could be effective in treating major depressive disorder. Additionally, research in The Journal of Alternative and Complementary Medicine (2021) found that vagus nerve stimulation through specific breathing exercises could improve mood and cognitive function, highlighting the therapeutic potential of breath in mental health interventions.

ENDOCRINE SYSTEM AND HORMONES

Breathwork practices can have a significant impact on the endocrine system, which is responsible for producing and regulating hormones in the body that affect our metabolism and overall health. The endocrine system is closely connected to the nervous system, and changes in the nervous system can affect the functioning of the endocrine system. Stressful breathing patterns, such as rapid and shallow breaths, can trigger the release of stress hormones like cortisol. Chronic stress, characterized by elevated cortisol levels, has been linked to a host of health issues, including hypertension, diabetes, and immune system suppression. Conversely, slow and controlled breathing can help modulate hormone levels.

Scientific Insights: A study in The International Journal of Yoga* (2020) assessed the effects of pranayama (a form of controlled breathing) on stress and cortisol levels. The findings revealed that regular practice of pranayama led to significant reductions in cortisol and improvements in stress-related symptoms. Research published in *Psychoneuroendocrinology* suggests that practices like slow breathing and meditation can lower cortisol levels and enhance overall endocrine balance. By engaging in practices that focus on deep breathing, individuals can foster a more resilient hormonal environment and therefore improve stress management and overall well-being.

In addition, breathwork practices that involve breath retention, such as pranayama techniques, can increase the levels of carbon dioxide in the blood. This can stimulate the respiratory center in the brainstem, which in turn can activate the hypothalamic-pituitary-adrenal (HPA) axis, a key regulator of the endocrine system. The HPA axis can influence the release of hormones such as cortisol, as well as other hormones such as growth hormone and thyroid hormones.

NEUROTRANSMITTERS

Breathing patterns can also affect neurotransmitter levels, the chemical messengers that facilitate communication within the brain. For instance, deep, rhythmic breathing can influence the balance of neurotransmitters such as serotonin and dopamine, which are critical for mood regulation and emotional stability. Nestor's exploration into breath reveals that controlled breathing can stimulate the release of endorphins, natural mood enhancers that contribute to a sense of well-being.

Scientific Insights: A study published in The Journal of Clinical Psychology* (2018) found that practices involving controlled breathing and meditation could increase GABA levels and reduce symptoms of anxiety and depression. The research highlighted the potential of breath-focused interventions to enhance neurotransmitter balance and improve mental health. Another study in The Journal of Alternative and Complementary Medicine* (2022) examined the effects of breathwork on endorphin levels. The results indicated that deep, intentional breathing could elevate endorphin levels, contributing to improved mood and emotional well-being.

THE MODERN-DAY SUPERHUMAN

Swami Rama's Experiment at Kansas University

In the 1970s, Swami Rama, a renowned yogi and master of meditation, undertook a groundbreaking experiment at the University of Kansas Medical Center. His objective was to demonstrate the extent of control a person could have over physiological processes through the power of breath and meditation.

Swami Rama was observed by a team of medical researchers led by Dr. Richard J. Davidson. During the experiment, Swami Rama entered a meditative state and was able to voluntarily regulate his autonomic nervous system, which typically operates outside of conscious control. This included slowing his heart rate, altering his blood pressure, and even changing the temperature of his hands. Remarkably, he could do all this while maintaining a deep meditative state.

The findings were revolutionary. They suggested that, through breath control and meditation, individuals could exert significant influence over bodily functions that were previously thought to be involuntary. Swami Rama's demonstration provided scientific validation to ancient yogic practices, highlighting the breath's profound impact on both mental and physical health.

In recent years, Wim Hof, also known as "The Iceman," has captivated the world with his extraordinary ability to withstand extreme conditions. Hof's method, known as the Wim Hof Method, combines specific breathing techniques, cold exposure, and meditation. His feats extend beyond mere endurance; they showcase the remarkable power of breath control in extreme situations.

One of Hof's most notable achievements was his ascent of Mount Everest in 2007. Although he did not reach the summit, he successfully climbed to 7,400 meters (24,300 feet) in shorts, an impressive feat given the harsh cold and thin air. Hof's ability to endure such extreme cold and altitude is attributed to his unique breathing techniques and mental conditioning, which help him regulate his body temperature and oxygen levels under severe conditions.

In addition to his mountain-climbing achievements, Hof has demonstrated his breath control capabilities in desert environments. In 2018, he ran a half marathon (21 kilometers or 13 miles) barefoot in the Namibian desert. The extreme heat and arid conditions make this feat particularly challenging. Hof's ability to maintain performance and manage body temperature in such environments further underscores the power of his breathing method.

Lastly, in a study conducted at the Radboud University Medical Center in the Netherlands, Hof and a group of practitioners underwent rigorous testing. The study aimed to assess the effects of Hof's breathing techniques on the immune system. Participants were exposed to a bacterial endotoxin to induce an inflammatory response. Remarkably, those who practiced Hof's breathing method showed a significantly reduced inflammatory response compared to a control group.

Both Swami Rama's experiment and Wim Hof's method offer compelling evidence of the profound effects controlled breathing can have on the body and mind. In conclusion, by harnessing the power of breath, we can foster a state of balance and well-being, allowing us to navigate life's challenges with greater resilience and ease. Remember that each inhalation and exhalation is an opportunity to harmonize the body's intricate systems and embrace a healthier, more mindful existence.

YOUR BREATH, YOUR POWER

The mind-body-breath connection is not just a theory—it is a lived experience you can access at any moment. Each breath you take carries the potential to heal, transform, and awaken you to a deeper understanding of yourself. By becoming more mindful of your breath, you can begin to harness its power, creating a ripple effect that touches every aspect of your life.

The journey of breath is a journey back to yourself. It's about reclaiming the innate wisdom of your body and using it to navigate the complexities of modern life with grace and ease. The breath is your ally, your guide, and your most accessible tool for creating balance, resilience, and well-being. So, take a deep breath, trust in the process, and let the power of your breath guide you to a life of greater health, harmony, and happiness.

HEAL YOUR PAST

Our past is not just a collection of memories; it is a powerful force that shapes every aspect of our lives. Without realizing it, we often carry the weight of old wounds, traumas, and unprocessed emotions, which silently dictate our thoughts, behaviors, and relationships. Whether it's a painful breakup, childhood neglect, a major loss, or even subtle experiences of not being seen or heard, these events leave an imprint on our bodies and minds. Over time, these unhealed parts of us can manifest as anxiety, depression, chronic stress, and self-sabotaging patterns, keeping us stuck in cycles of pain.

Living with unhealed trauma is like dragging an invisible anchor through life. It slows us down, keeps us tethered to old fears, and blocks us from experiencing the freedom, joy, and fulfilment we deeply crave. You may have felt this yourself—the persistent anxiety that nags at you, the inner critic that never seems to be satisfied, or the emotional numbness that keeps you from fully engaging with life. But what if I told you that healing your past doesn't require years of therapy or reliving every painful memory? What if you could begin the process of releasing the past and reclaiming your power with something as simple as your breath?

UNDERSTANDING TRAUMA: MORE THAN JUST A MEMORY

Trauma is not just a singular event; it's a complex experience that imprints itself in our cells and psyche. It represents the body's response to overwhelming events or experiences, leaving behind traces that impact us physiologically, psychologically, and energetically. Dr. Gabor Maté, a leading expert in trauma research, describes trauma as an "invisible force" that molds our lives and influences our perspectives, emotions, and physical health. He suggests that many of our mental, emotional, and physical challenges—such as addiction, depression, and chronic illnesses—are deeply rooted in early-life trauma that remains unaddressed. It's also important to note that a lot of new research in the realm of epigenetics is now emerging, showing how trauma can be passed down through our gene pool. This may explain why some people who never experienced severe trauma as a child still display certain emotional behaviors, coping mechanisms, or stress responses as if they had experienced intense trauma.

The effects of trauma are evident both on personal and global scales. From individual experiences to widespread issues like violence, war, and economic disparity, trauma leaves deep scars. The rise of digital media has exacerbated this, with constant exposure to global tragedies through news and social media creating secondary traumatic stress or "compassion fatigue." This deluge of information has desensitized us to suffering, contributing to a rise in mental health issues and societal divisions, as well as a pervasive sense of disconnection and numbness. Understanding the pervasive nature of trauma is essential not only to address visible symptoms but also to heal the underlying wounds and foster a society focused on resilience, compassion, and holistic well-being. Regardless of who you are, no one escapes this human experience without some form of wounding.

TYPES OF TRAUMA

Trauma varies in degrees, yet all forms can have lasting effects.

- **Acute Trauma:** Results from a single incident, such as a car accident or sudden loss.
- **Chronic Trauma:** Arises from repeated and prolonged exposure to highly stressful events, such as ongoing physical, psychological, emotional, or sexual abuse, domestic violence; attachment disruptions like inconsistent or unresponsive caregiving; lack of affection, emotional support, or attention; and cultural or racial discrimination.
- **Complex Trauma:** Involves exposure to multiple traumatic events, often of an invasive and interpersonal nature.

THE NEGATIVE IMPACT OF TRAUMA

Trauma triggers the body's stress response, often leading to chronic hyper-vigilance. This state of alertness results in one of four trauma responses:

- **Fight:** This response involves confronting the threat directly. Individuals may become aggressive or confrontational as a way to defend themselves or assert control over the situation. This is often driven by adrenaline and can be beneficial in actual dangerous situations but problematic if misdirected.
- **Flight:** This involves escaping the threat as quickly as possible. People may physically flee or may withdraw emotionally, avoiding confrontation or any reminders of the trauma.
- **Freeze:** In a freeze response, individuals may find themselves physically unable to move or act. They feel

paralyzed, as if their bodies have shut down in the face of overwhelming threat. This can also manifest as being "stuck" in certain emotions or thought patterns related to the trauma.
- **Fawn:** A lesser-known response, fawning involves attempting to appease or please others to avoid conflict or further threats. People who "fawn" might go out of their way to satisfy others or make concessions at their own expense, often neglecting their own needs.

This heightened state disrupts natural bodily rhythms, including breath, leading to chronic health issues, anxiety, and difficulties in forming connections. Psychologically, trauma distorts our self-perception and worldview, often resulting in feelings of helplessness and worthlessness. Memories of trauma may surface as flashbacks or nightmares, and if these emotions remain unprocessed, they create core wounds that contribute to physical and mental health issues, unhealthy behaviors, and sabotaged relationships.

Some of the most common patterns, emotions, and behaviors that one may experience as a result of unhealed trauma include:

- Anxiety, stress, depression, and PTSD
- Fear of rejection, abandonment, and uncertainty
- Low self-esteem and feelings of unworthiness
- Addiction to substances or compulsive behaviors
- Emotional disconnection and a pervasive sense of unsafety
- Self-blame, criticism, and people-pleasing tendencies
- Obsessive thinking and a lack of authenticity

If we want to create the life we desire, we must first heal our past. That begins by bringing awareness to what we've endured and experienced without becoming victims of our circumstances. By illuminating all the painful parts of ourselves and the areas within us that need attention, love, and acceptance, we can begin to transmute our deepest wounds into our greatest power. Although I'm not saying anyone deserves to go through violent or painful experiences, from a soul perspective, we have chosen to incarnate into this "earth school" and into this realm of separation with one intention: to learn, grow, and evolve. Therefore, from this vantage point, our trauma can be used as an evolutionary catalyst. When we heal ourselves, we heal the collective.

MARIA'S STORY: FROM WOUNDED TO WHOLE

Maria has always been driven. As a leading brand and marketing specialist in her mid-thirties, she has a sharp intellect and relentless ambition. Yet, beneath her polished exterior, Maria constantly battles a storm of persistent fear and anxiety she can't seem to outrun. Despite her achievements, she often feels like an imposter in her own life, plagued by a nagging sense of unworthiness. Yoga and therapy offer little relief. Her nights are plagued by echoes of the past, and she feels increasingly isolated from those she loves. Soon, she withdrew from those she loved, feeling increasingly isolated and misunderstood. On the outside, she maintained her composed façade, but inside, she was unraveling. When she reached out for help, it was clear she carried a burden of repressed energy.

During our initial conversation, I observed a tense body and an overactive mind stuck in story loops about how the world was out to get her. She was constantly on edge, as if bracing for an attack that never came. Her mind was stuck in an endless loop of stories about betrayal, abandonment, and how the world was out to get her—a narrative shaped by years of pain she had never fully processed.

As we began to explore her past, Maria hesitantly opened up about the painful details of her childhood. Orphaned by a tragic accident that claimed her parents' lives when she was just a young girl, she had been shuffled from one foster home to another, never staying long enough to form real bonds or feel truly safe. Each new home brought a wave of uncertainty, and Maria quickly learned that the only person she could rely on was herself. This early abandonment left a profound wound that she carried into adulthood, manifesting in her relationships and daily interactions. Though she appeared composed, the trauma of her early years had trapped her in a cycle of self-sabotage, where she constantly doubted her worth and feared that those she loved would one day leave her, just as her parents had.

In her romantic relationships, she often found herself on high alert, interpreting even the slightest conflict as a sign she was about to be abandoned. She built emotional walls that kept her partner at a distance, convinced that if she let anyone too close, they would see the broken parts of her she worked so hard to hide. Professionally, Maria poured herself into her work, using her career as both a shield and a distraction from her internal pain. She excelled because she needed to prove, at least to herself, that she was capable and worthy, yet the relentless pursuit of success left her feeling even more disconnected and exhausted.

In the months that followed, we embarked on a journey of healing that involved various somatic and emotional healing methods (many of which I share in this chapter), with breathwork being a crucial component. Through each session, she was able to access and release layers of stagnant energy stored in her body for years. The process was not easy; there were tears, tremors, and moments of deep emotional release as she reconnected with parts of herself she had long buried. The act of breathing became a means of reconnecting with parts of herself she had long neglected. Week by week, she noticed tangible improvements, and the constant anxiety that once shadowed her life began to recede.

As she peeled back the layers, the changes in her life were profound. Her interactions with her partner became more open, honest, and vulnerable. She allowed herself to be seen, flaws and all, and in doing so, deepened her connection in ways she had never thought possible. With friends, she was no longer the guarded, distant observer but an active participant in her own life, engaging with others from a place of authenticity and trust. Professionally, Maria experienced a renaissance of creativity and focus. No longer driven by fear, she found genuine fulfillment in her work and began to take on new challenges with confidence. Her career soared as she took on a leadership role that once would have terrified her. She was promoted to an executive position, earning five times her previous salary. She no longer used her work as a way to outrun her past; instead, she embraced it as a platform to express her true potential. Maria's story is a powerful reminder that when we heal our past, we free ourselves to step into a future that feels expansive, authentic, and truly our own.

IT'S ALL IN THE BODY

The human body is a highly intelligent system that holds within it the stories of our lives, including every experience, emotion, and memory. Our bodies are constantly interacting with and adapting to the world around us, and as a result, they become repositories of information. Dr. Peter Levine, a renowned psychologist, trauma expert, and author, emphasizes that trauma is both a psychological and physiological event that becomes stored in the body. This storage of trauma can cause dysregulation in the nervous system, resulting in a person feeling stuck in fight, flight, or freeze responses long after the traumatic event has ended. In his book "Walking the Tiger," he shares that by tuning into our bodily sensations, we can gain insight into our experiences and work towards greater self-awareness, regulation, resilience, and healing. His technique and practice, Somatic Experiencing, involves gently guiding individuals to reconnect with sensations that have been suppressed or from which they have dissociated due to trauma. By allowing the body to re-experience these sensations in a controlled and safe way, the nervous system can reset, and the traumatic energy can be discharged.

In nature, animals naturally discharge the energy of a traumatic event through shaking, movement, or other physical responses. Humans, however, often suppress these natural responses due to societal norms or internalized fears, leading to unprocessed trauma.

Therefore, Somatic Experiencing helps individuals access and complete these responses, releasing stored tension and trauma from the body as a result of completing the trauma cycle.

❖ EXERCISE 1: BODY SCAN MEDITATION

Below, you'll find a body scan meditation that will support you in bringing awareness to the sensations present within you. You can have someone read this aloud to you or use the recorded audio on the "Beats and Breath" app.

Begin by making yourself comfortable. Sit in a chair and allow your back to be straight, but not stiff, with your feet planted on the ground beneath you. If you have back problems, you can do this practice lying down with your head supported.

Place one hand on your belly and one hand on your heart and allow your eyes to close.

Take several long, slow, deep breaths in through your nose and out through your mouth. Feel your stomach expand first, and then allow your heart to expand on an inhale and relax as you exhale.

Simply notice the rise and fall of each breath and any sensations that may be arising in your body without judgment.

Now begin to drop your hands onto your lap or by your side and draw your awareness and attention to the bottom of your feet. Simply notice the feelings throughout your feet, including your sole, heel, toes, and the top of the foot.

Travel up your body, noticing the sensations in your ankles, shins, and calves. Notice sensations both deep in the muscles and on the surface of your skin.

As you breathe in and out, continue to become aware of the feelings in your legs as you move up to your knees and thighs. Notice how your clothing feels against your skin.

Moving up your body, take note of the feelings in your quads, hamstrings, and hips. Simply notice the feelings without any need to change them.

Pay attention to the feelings in your lower back. Notice how your body feels against the surface on which you are sitting or lying down.

Draw your awareness around your belly and abdomen. This is where many of us store worry, stress, and anxiety. Simply observe this entire region as your belly rises and falls with each inhale and exhale.

Raise this energy into your chest, experiencing any sensations in your heart space. Move your breath into your heart, noticing your heartbeat or any other feelings arising within you.

Now send your breath into the middle of your back or the other side of your heart. Observing, feeling, allowing.

Move up into your upper back, shoulders, and neck, breathing and releasing with each inhale and exhale.

Allow your awareness to move down your arms, into your elbows, forearms, wrists, and hands. Breathe in and out through your fingertips.

Drawing this energy up your arms and through your neck into your jaw, allow your jaw to loosen and release with every breath you take.

Now into your cheeks and ears. Allow your awareness to move into your eyes and into the space between your eyes.

Move your awareness up into the center of your forehead, around to your temples, and finally around the circumference of your head.

Finally, slowly scan your entire body, noticing all the sensations from your toes to the top of your head.

What do you feel? What sensations arose for you? Where did you feel them?

Stay here for a few more moments and simply notice and breathe.

To close out this practice, repeat after me...

I direct, instruct, command, and compel my body, organs, tissues, muscles, and cells to be restored to their original state of wholeness right now. Thank you. And so it is.

By practicing this exercise, over time you will establish a new and profound connection with yourself, allowing you to begin releasing the stored and stagnant energy caught within your body. Once we have created a more harmonious relationship with our body through breath awareness and deep feeling, we can begin to work with the deeper parts of ourselves.

BRINGING LIGHT TO THE DARKNESS

We must shine a light on all the painful parts of ourselves and the areas within us that require our love, attention, and acceptance. To do so, we must turn toward our shadow. The shadow is the part of the human psyche composed of all the elements a person represses or denies about themselves. It includes the traits, emotions, and behaviors a person deems unacceptable or unlovable and which are, therefore, kept hidden in the unconscious. Our personal shadow is formed through a combination of factors, including societal conditioning, trauma, cultural influences and internal, genetic imprints.

Coined by Swiss psychologist Carl Jung, "shadow work" is a psychological process that involves exploring and understanding the darker aspects of the self to integrate them into one's consciousness and improve overall well-being. It is a process of self-exploration and self-awareness that involves bringing to consciousness the parts of ourselves we have repressed or denied. Therefore by bringing our unconscious patterns and emotions into the light of our awareness, we can better understand ourselves and liberate our unique gifts and creative genius as well as become a more whole and authentic version of ourselves.

❖ EXERCISE 2: EMOTIONAL EXPRESSION EXERCISE

One of the most important steps in shadow work is to identify and feel the emotions we have repressed. The word "emotion" dates back to the 16th century from the Old French "emouvoir," meaning "to stir up," and Latin "emovere," meaning "move out, remove, agitate." Emotion, then, represents "movement." In other words, emotions are simply movements of energy. The problem is that we haven't been taught how to process our emotions, at least not in a healthy and safe manner. Most of us have grown accustomed to either suppressing them or personifying them so intensely because our primary caregivers never taught us how to express them, nor did they give us the space to do so. As a result, we fall into the trap of clinging to them, so they become an integral extension of who we are. Hence, we mistake our emotions for our identity—we allow them to define us.

Emotions are divine messengers. They are inner wisdom within us. They manifest physically and provide us with vital information about what we are experiencing and what actions we need to take. Emotions are an essential part of what we are as human beings, but they're not who we are. Yes, they can be messy, complicated, and confusing, but they're not there to control your life; they're there to guide you forward on your path.

Each of the emotions we experience has an origin point within the body. In fact, in Traditional Chinese Medicine (TCM), each trapped emotion can be traced back to a specific organ within the body. By learning the language of organs and the associated emotions stored within them, we can restore the self-healing mechanisms within otherwise dysfunctional parts of the body.

1. **The Heart (xin):** The Heart is associated with joy and happiness. An imbalance in this organ can lead to feelings of anxiety, restlessness, and insomnia. During your breathing practice, use the sound "Haww" on your exhale to open and lift the heart energy.

2. **The Liver (gan):** The Liver is associated with anger and frustration. An imbalance in this organ can lead to feelings of depression, irritability, and mood swings. During your breathing practice, use the sound "Shhh" on your exhale to promote the smooth flow of energy and blood to your liver.

3. **The Spleen (pi):** The Spleen is associated with worry and overthinking. An imbalance in this organ can lead to feelings of anxiety, fatigue, and a lack of focus. During your breathing practice, use the sound "Whoo" on your exhale to strengthen the Spleen and balance the emotion of worry.

4. **The Lungs (fei):** The Lungs are associated with grief and sadness. An imbalance in this organ can lead to feelings of anxiety, depression, and a weakened immune system. During your breathing practice, use the sound "Sss" on your exhale to strengthen and cleanse the Lungs.

5. **The Kidneys (shen):** The Kidneys are associated with fear and anxiety. An imbalance in this organ can lead to feelings of insecurity, phobias, and difficulty coping with stress. During your breathing practice, use the sound "Chooo" on your exhale to expel fear.

"You can have someone read this aloud to you, or you can find our 'Emotional Alchemy Series' on the Beats and Breath app."

Begin by sitting in a comfortable position.

Close your eyes and begin breathing deeply and slowly.

With every inhale and exhale, become attuned to the sensations you feel inside your body and allow them to guide you to any areas where you are holding tension and constriction.

Once you've identified the area of constriction, place your focus there and become aware of any emotion(s) that are present. Begin to ask yourself the following questions:

1. If (insert emotion) had a voice, what message would it share with me?
2. When did this emotion first become trapped in my body?

Just simply allow yourself to continue to breathe and sink into the feelings arising within you, using the associated exhale sound from the list above.

"Stay here as long as you need to feel fully relaxed."

HEALING THE CHILD WITHIN

The "inner child" refers to the emotional and psychological part of the self that represents one's childhood experiences and emotions. The inner child often holds onto memories, emotions, and feelings from childhood that influence one's thoughts, feelings, behaviors, and decisions in adulthood. Due to our trauma patterns, most of us have a wounded child within and thus experience many difficulties in life. By working with and reparenting our inner child, we begin to create the safety and security our younger selves have always needed, allowing the positive traits of our inner child to have room to shine in our present-day life experience. This leads to increased self-awareness, emotional stability, improved relationships, and the activation of our natural gifts. On the other hand, when we avoid addressing our past hurts and feel alone with them, they transform into behaviors destructive to ourselves and our environment.

❖ EXERCISE 3: INNER CHILD EXERCISE

Below are some steps to help you connect with your inner child. You can also find a dynamic "inner child" breathwork session on the Beats and Breath app.

1. **Imagine your inner child:** Visualize a younger version of yourself, specifically the part of yourself when these emotions became trapped as a result of a traumatic experience. It may help to have a picture of you from this time period. See the child as vividly as you can, with all the details of their physical appearance, clothing, and surroundings.

2. **Speak to your inner child:** Address your inner child and speak to them as you would to a real child. Ask them how they feel, what they need, and what they would like to tell you or express. Listen to the answers that come to you, even if they seem strange or unexpected. At times, they may want to scream or cry.

3. **Embrace and validate your inner child:** Acknowledge and validate the emotions, thoughts, and experiences of your inner child. Let them know that they are heard, seen, and loved. Offer them comfort and reassurance, and let them know it's safe to express their feelings.

4. **Create action steps:** In what ways can you two (yourself now and your inner child) become a team and work together? What are some safe places or spaces you can go to when you are feeling overwhelmed and need to recharge?

5. **Practice self-compassion:** Treat yourself with the same kindness and compassion you would offer to someone else. Remember that your inner child is a part of you and deserves to be treated with care and understanding.

6. **Repeat the process:** Connecting with your inner child can be a powerful experience, but it can also be challenging. It's important to approach it with patience and compassion and to repeat the process as often as you need to.

FREEDOM FROM SUFFERING

As we turn inward to heal our own wounds, we inadvertently set forth a tidal wave of healing that reaches far beyond the confines of our personal existence. This is why inner work is the most important work we can do. Each step we take on our journey of self-healing, discovery, and empowerment sends ripples into the vast ocean of human consciousness, touching lives, mending hearts, and subtly reshaping the world one breath at a time. This deep alchemical process of personal transformation not only nurtures our own spirit and soothes our scars, but contributes a silent yet powerful medicine that heals the soul of the world.

Imagine a tapestry woven with the threads of individual lives—each color, each strand representing a person's journey through the shadows and light of their existence. When one thread brightens with the light of healing, it does not simply change in isolation; it illuminates those entwined with it, enhancing the vibrancy of the whole. In this way, our personal healings are never purely personal—they are communal acts of love and restoration.

"HEALING IS A JOURNEY, NOT A DESTINATION."

Healing your past is not about erasing what happened or pretending it didn't affect you. It's about reclaiming your power and choosing to no longer be defined by your wounds. Breathwork provides a direct and gentle way to connect with your body, release trapped emotions, and rewire your nervous system. Each breath is an opportunity to rewrite your story, to move from victimhood to empowerment, and to transform your pain into purpose.

As you continue this journey of self-discovery, remember that healing is not linear. There will be ups and downs, moments of clarity, and moments of confusion. Be patient with yourself, honor your process, and trust that with each conscious breath, you are moving closer to the freedom and fulfillment you deserve.

Your past does not have to dictate your future. The power to heal lies within you, in every breath you take. So, take a deep breath, exhale the old, and make space for the new. You are not broken; you are becoming whole.

DISCOVER YOUR PURPOSE

Many of us carry a silent weight—a heaviness that clings to us just beneath the surface of our daily lives. It lingers in the quiet moments when the noise fades, and we are left alone with our thoughts. It's the nagging sense that something vital is missing, an emptiness that no amount of work, relationships, or achievements can fill. It's waking up with a hollow feeling in your chest, the sense that you're merely existing rather than truly living, drifting through days that feel disconnected from any real meaning.

This disconnection from your deeper sense of purpose is not just a minor inconvenience; it's a profound mental, emotional, and spiritual ache. It gnaws at you in ways you can't always articulate—a low hum of discontent that seeps into everything you do. It steals the joy from moments that should feel fulfilling, turns achievements into empty milestones, and relationships into shallow connections. This void often manifests as anxiety, a restless sadness, or a constant undercurrent of unease, as if you are perpetually out of sync with the rhythm of your own life. It's a slow erosion of joy, where the things that once sparked excitement now feel like burdens, leaving you numb and yearning for something you can't quite name.

Living without purpose feels like being adrift in a vast, fog-covered landscape where each day blurs into the next, indistinguishable from the last. You might catch yourself chasing fleeting moments of happiness—scrolling through social media, binge-watching shows, buying things you don't need—grasping at anything that might momentarily distract you from the ache you feel inside. But despite your best efforts to drown it out, the emptiness lingers, a stark and constant reminder that something essential is missing. It feels like standing on the edge of a precipice, paralyzed by the fear of taking a step in any direction because you are overwhelmed by choices and unable to find a clear path forward. The fog of self-doubt thickens, making it hard to see who you are or where you are meant to go.

Emotionally, it's like carrying a weight that drags at your heart, a quiet desperation that whispers questions in the dark: "Is this all there is? Why am I here? What's the point of it all?" The answers seem just out of reach, hidden behind a curtain of expectations, obligations, and the relentless pressure to be someone you're not. The ache of purposelessness isn't just a feeling—it's a constant tug at your soul, pulling you away from the life you were meant to live and leaving you stranded in a place of unfulfilled potential. You're alive, but not truly living, caught in the endless loop of autopilot, longing for something more but unsure how to find it.

THE ILLUSION OF THE "ONE TRUE PURPOSE"

Many of us feel an immense pressure to find our "one true purpose," as if there's a single path that will bring us ultimate fulfillment. We search for signs, seek guidance, and sometimes get caught in a loop of self-doubt, wondering if we're on the "right" track. But the idea that we have just one fixed purpose can be paralyzing. It suggests that our value is tied to a specific role, job, or achievement, and that if we miss it, we have somehow failed. The truth is that purpose is not a destination—it's a way of being. It's not about what you do, but how you show up in the world. Your purpose can evolve as you grow, change, and learn more about yourself. It's less about finding the perfect answer and more about embracing the questions, exploring your curiosities, and following the threads of what lights you up.

THE COMPASS OF THE SOUL

Purpose is not a luxury; it's the very heartbeat of our well-being. It's the quiet but powerful force that pulls us out of bed each morning, whispers resilience in the face of adversity, and drives us to push beyond our limits toward something greater than ourselves. Without purpose, we are left adrift, lost in the vast expanse of daily life, searching for meaning in a world that can often feel indifferent and overwhelming. Purpose is the compass that guides us. It transforms our existence from mere survival into a journey of thriving, fueling us with a sense of significance that transcends the mundane.

Our higher purpose is the "north star" that provides direction when all else feels uncertain, illuminating our path even in the darkest of times. It's the driving force behind our most courageous choices and greatest achievements, lighting the way when everything else seems dim. Purpose is not some grand, elusive mission we must struggle to invent; it's an organic extension of who we are when we peel back the layers of societal expectations, fears, and self-doubt. It reveals itself in moments of our excitement, in tasks that make time stand still, and in the effortless connections we make with others. It's in the warmth of a smile, the act of helping a friend, and in the passions that set your soul on fire.

Finding purpose isn't about chasing something external or waiting for a life-changing revelation. It's an inner calling, an essence that has always been there, whispering softly beneath the noise of daily life, waiting for you to pause and listen. It asks you to reflect on deeper questions: What is your reason for being? What unique gifts do you possess that are meant to be shared with the world? Purpose is the realization that you are here for a reason, that your existence is not random—it's intentional. And when you connect with that purpose, you tap into an infinite well of energy and motivation, a powerful force that propels you into service of something far greater than yourself.

Purpose transforms the ordinary into the extraordinary. It's the sacred thread that weaves through every aspect of your life, binding together your experiences, passions, and dreams into a tapestry that is uniquely yours. It's the profound awareness that your life matters, that you have something invaluable to offer, and that the world is brighter because you are here. Purpose isn't just about what you do; it's about who you become when you choose to live with intention, authenticity, and a deep connection to your soul's calling.

FROM DISSATISFACTION TO FULFILLMENT

For years, Mark ignored the subtle signs of dissatisfaction. He believed that if he worked harder, achieved more, and reached the next goal, he would finally feel fulfilled. So he climbed the ranks quickly, earning accolades, bonuses, and the lifestyle that many would envy. But the promotions and raises only provided temporary highs, which were followed by deeper and deeper lows. Mark described his life as being stuck on a "hamster wheel"—moving but going nowhere. His health began to suffer; he experienced frequent anxiety, insomnia, and a pervasive sense of burnout that no vacation seemed to cure. Despite his outward success, Mark felt as if he were slowly losing himself.

The breaking point came when he found himself unable to focus during a critical meeting. His mind was clouded, his motivation gone, and he felt completely disconnected from the work that used to define him. That night, Mark sat in his luxury high-rise apartment, staring out at the city lights, and realized that despite all his achievements, he had no idea what truly mattered to him anymore. He was tired of pretending to be someone he no longer recognized and knew he needed a change, but he didn't know where to begin.

Mark reached out to me after he was introduced to my work from a corporate breathwork session I led a few months earlier. During our initial consultation, it was clear that Mark's struggles went far beyond job dissatisfaction—he was experiencing an existential crisis. He felt trapped in a life that looked perfect on the outside but was devoid of meaning on the inside. Mark was eager to find a sense of direction but skeptical of anything outside the corporate framework he had lived in for 22 years.

We began our work by first getting to the root of his dissatisfaction, helping him reconnect with his body and feelings. In our first few sessions, he was struck by how emotional he felt—something he hadn't allowed himself to experience in years. Like most men in modern society, he had been numbing himself, while beneath the surface was a well of suppressed feelings, memories, and insights.

As Mark delved deeper, he began to uncover the patterns that had shaped his life—both the shadows that held him back and the gifts that lay dormant within him. We worked with various self-healing and mastery tools, including "Gene Keys," breathwork, and somatic experiencing, to illuminate his natural-born talents as well as where he had been playing small out of fear and conditioning. He realized that his drive for success had been fueled by a need for external validation rather than a true connection to his inner purpose.

Session by session, we released the physical tension stored in Mark's body from years of stress and unexpressed emotions, allowing him to feel more grounded and present and helping him tune into his own intuition and desires. As a result, he started to understand how his body held the stories of his past.

During one specific session, he had a breakthrough. He described seeing himself standing at a crossroads, with one path leading back to his familiar corporate life and the other into unknown territory. For the first time, he felt a deep pull toward the latter—a path that wasn't about status or financial gain, but about creating something that truly mattered to him. Mark began to see his work not as an end in itself, but as a vehicle for making a positive impact on others.

Over time, Mark made the courageous decision to step back from his high-powered role and explore new avenues that aligned with his values. He started volunteering with a local nonprofit, mentoring young entrepreneurs, and even launched a podcast where he shared his journey of rediscovering purpose. The skills and insights he gained from our sessions helped him redefine success on his own terms and allowed him to feel more connected to his body's wisdom, guiding him through moments of doubt and fear. Today, Mark describes his life as fulfilling in a way he never thought possible. He currently does personal coaching for leaders and entrepreneurs, supporting them to heal and create an impact in the world while earning just as much as he did in his previous executive role.

❖ EXERCISE: UNLOCKING PURPOSE

Breath is one of the most powerful ways to unlock purpose because it draws us into a state of presence and coherence. When we are fully present, we are no longer caught up in the stories of the past or the anxieties of the future. In this stillness, we can hear the subtle whispers of our intuition, guiding us toward what is most meaningful and aligned with our soul's desires. By centering ourselves through the breath, we release resistance, dissolve fear, and cultivate the trust needed to walk the path of our purpose with clarity and conviction while creating the inner space necessary to connect with the core of who we are and what we are meant to bring into the world.

Locate the "Purpose" Breathwork session on the Beats and Breath app and find a comfortable, quiet place for the next 30 to 60 minutes where you can be by yourself and with your breath. As you breathe into this moment, allow yourself to feel the pulse of your inner calling. Let it stir something deep inside you, awakening the dormant parts of your soul. You are not here to simply go through the motions; you are here to create, to love, to serve, and to lead a life rich with meaning and impact.

Afterward, take time to journal on the following questions:

What did you feel or experience during the breathwork journey?
What insights or clarity arose for you?
How can you put this clarity into action?
What small step can you take today to begin aligning your actions with the clarity you gained?

Discovering your purpose is a deeply personal and evolving journey. As you stand on the edge of this new beginning, trust in the unfolding of your path. Trust that the whispers of your soul will guide you and that your inner purpose will reveal itself in perfect timing. You are here for a reason. Trust that reason, embrace your purpose, and step fully into the life you were born to live.

EXPAND YOUR CONSCIOUSNESS

Life is more than just a series of events; it's a continuous journey of transformation. Throughout our lives, we're constantly going through cycles of death and rebirth, not in the physical sense, but on a deeper, metaphysical level. To grow and expand into greater versions of ourselves, we must be willing to let go of the old identities that no longer serve us. Just as a caterpillar goes through a metamorphosis, surrendering its cocoon to become a butterfly, we too must release our old self, allowing the wings of our true potential to unfold and carry us into something new.

This transformation isn't about becoming someone else; it's about stripping away layers of conditioning to reveal who we truly are. It's a rebirth, a coming home to the deeper love, joy, wholeness, and prosperity that have always been within us. As we let go, we begin to see the world through fresh eyes, feeling more alive, aligned, and connected to our authentic truth.

These cycles of dying to the old and embracing the new are continuous invitations to step beyond our comfort zones into the unknown. It takes courage to surrender to this process, trusting that each ending paves the way for something better. By embracing these cycles, we honor our growth, seeing every death as a doorway, every challenge as a chance to evolve, and every surrender as a step closer to authenticity. We become the alchemists of our own lives, transmuting pain into wisdom, fear into freedom, and limitation into possibility.

MY DARK NIGHT OF THE SOUL

At the beginning of 2022, I found myself in a dark place. After years of inner work, service, and growth, it felt like I was back at square one. For three agonizing weeks, I couldn't muster the strength to get out of bed. The vibrant purpose that had once fueled my days seemed to vanish overnight, replaced by a suffocating depression that wrapped itself around me like a heavy cloak. It wasn't just sadness—it was an all-encompassing numbness that left me feeling hollow, disconnected, and adrift.

Each day bled into the next, the minutes dragging on with an unbearable weight. The world outside continued to turn, but I was stuck, paralyzed by a despair I couldn't fully understand. Friends and loved ones reached out, but their words fell flat, unable to penetrate the fog that clouded my mind. I felt lost, as if I were trapped in a never-ending night with no dawn in sight. I was experiencing what many refer to as the "dark night of the soul"—a profound period of desolation and inner turmoil that strips away everything you thought you knew about yourself.

This wasn't the first time I'd faced darkness, but it was the first time it felt so absolute. I knew I needed something more—something radical to break through the barriers that were keeping me trapped in this void. I needed to confront the darkness head-on, to dive deep into the shadows that had surfaced within me. That's when I came across the concept of a dark room retreat—a prolonged time of isolation in complete darkness, designed to facilitate deep introspection, heightened awareness, and spiritual transformation.

ENTERING THE DARKNESS

Embarking on a dark room retreat felt like both a terrifying leap and an inevitable step. I was drawn to the idea of immersing myself in complete blackness for five straight days, stripped of all external distractions. My intentions were clear: to delve deeply into the recesses of my inner self, test my discipline and faith, and face my deepest shadows. It was a journey I knew I needed, but I was unprepared for the intensity that awaited me.

The moment the door closed and the last sliver of light disappeared, I was plunged into a darkness so profound that it seemed to press in on me from all sides. My senses, so used to constant stimulation, were thrown into disarray. Time lost all meaning; minutes felt like hours, and days blurred together in an endless cycle of waking and sleeping. I was left alone with nothing but my thoughts—a self-imposed prison that held up a mirror to every fear, doubt, and unresolved wound I carried.

The first two days were a brutal confrontation with my own mind. Without the usual distractions of light, sound, and activity, my thoughts became louder and more relentless. I found myself consumed by a visceral fear of death—an irrational yet overpowering terror that I wouldn't make it through this experience. My ego fought hard, urging me to abandon the darkness and return to the familiar comforts of the outside world. Every moment was a battle, a test of my will to stay present with the discomfort.

On the third day, when I felt like I could no longer endure, something shifted. Exhausted and defeated, I made a choice to surrender completely to the process. I stopped fighting the darkness and allowed myself to sink into it, embracing the unknown with a trust I hadn't felt in a long time. In that surrender, the true transformation began.

THE EMERGENCE OF INNER LIGHT

As I moved deeper into the experience, the darkness that once felt suffocating began to change. It became a nurturing space—a cocoon that held me as I unraveled. My body and mind found a rhythm in the stillness, and the constant chatter of my ego slowly faded. In the absence of light, my soul's voice grew clearer, guiding me toward a profound inner wisdom. I started to see flickers of light within my mind's eye—tiny fractals that danced like ethereal fireflies across the vast black canvas of my consciousness.

These light fractals wove through my inner landscape, reminiscent of my first ayahuasca ceremony in the Ecuadorian Amazon in late 2016, where I glimpsed alternate dimensions of reality. This time, however, the light felt deeply personal. It traveled up and down my spine, illuminating and clearing energetic blockages within me. I sensed these lights interacting with my DNA, unlocking strands that had long been dormant, as if I were witnessing the very essence of my being coming alive.

The darkness wasn't just an absence of light; it was a space of profound potential, a gateway to higher states of consciousness. The blackness became a mirror reflecting the light within, revealing parts of myself I had forgotten. It was as though I had been granted a front-row seat to my own transformation—a celestial light show orchestrated by my breath and guided by my inner knowing.

When the retreat finally ended, I emerged a changed man. The journey had pushed me to the edges of my sanity, but it was also the most liberating experience of my life. The darkness stripped me down to my core, forcing me to confront my deepest shadows, and in doing so, reignited a light within me that I didn't know was still there. I felt renewed, not just in my mind but in my very soul, ready to step deeper into my mission and share my insights and transformations with the world.

BREATH: A GATEWAY TO HIGHER CONSCIOUSNESS

In the silence of the dark room, I discovered that my breath was not just my anchor but a gateway through which I could reconnect with the light within and enhance my intuitive abilities. The breath holds profound power, and it is through conscious breathing that we can dispel darkness, elevate our vibrational energy, and open ourselves to new dimensions of awareness.

In ancient Hindu tradition, the Rishis—sages and seers who authored the Vedas—knew this well. The Rishis were said to have received the Vedic knowledge directly from the divine, and they transmitted these revelations to humanity in the form of hymns, mantras, and sacred texts.

According to Vedic lore, the Rishis once consumed a sacred drink called "soma," a psychoactive elixir mentioned in ancient texts. Although the exact nature of soma remains uncertain, it is believed to have been either cannabis or mushroom-based. Soma was reputed to induce euphoria, heightened awareness, and a deep connection to the universal energies, offering direct insights into the Akasha, or the "book of life." It was also said to possess healing properties.

Eventually, the Rishis could no longer produce soma and thus sought alternative means to reach similar states of consciousness. They turned their focus to their breathing, developing sophisticated breathing techniques as a replacement for the soma brew. Through conscious modulation of their breath, they discovered they could achieve profound shifts in consciousness, gain insight, and experience states of bliss and cosmic unity that rivaled and often surpassed those induced by the sacred drink. These practices laid the groundwork for what we now know as pranayama, demonstrating the power of breath as a tool for spiritual and metaphysical exploration.

THE METAPHYSICS OF BREATHING

In the ancient yogic tradition, the human body transcends its physical form, embodying a complex system of energy. This subtle anatomy, foundational to both yoga and Ayurveda, reveals a map for our journey into expanded consciousness. Central to this map is a network of energy channels, or nadis, through which prana flows, nurturing the body, mind, and spirit. Ancient texts describe 72,000 nadis, but three stand out: Ida, Pingala, and Sushumna.

- **Ida Nadi**: Located on the left side of the spine, Ida is associated with lunar energy, the feminine principle, and the parasympathetic nervous system. It governs the right hemisphere of the brain, which is linked to intuition, creativity, and emotions.
- **Pingala Nadi**: On the right side of the spine lies Pingala, which is associated with solar energy, the masculine principle, and the sympathetic nervous system. It governs the left hemisphere of the brain, which is linked to logic, reason, and analytical thinking.
- **Sushumna Nadi**: Running along the central axis of the spine, Sushumna is the primary channel for spiritual awakening. When kundalini energy is awakened, it rises through this nadi, leading to the union of Ida and Pingala energies and the transcendence of duality.

Breathing practices, or pranayama, are essential for purifying and balancing the nadis. When the nadis are clear, prana flows freely, stilling the mind, invigorating the body, and uplifting the spirit. Thus, the breath becomes a vehicle for moving prana through these subtle channels, guiding us toward higher states of consciousness.

CHAKRAS: WHEELS OF LIGHT

Along the sushumna nadi lie the seven major chakras, often visualized as spinning wheels of light. Each chakra corresponds to different aspects of our physical, emotional, and spiritual being. From the root chakra at the base of the spine to the crown chakra at the top of the head, these energy centers form a ladder of consciousness. As we engage in specific breathing techniques, we can activate and harmonize these chakras, gradually ascending from earthly awareness to cosmic consciousness. As prana flows through the nadis, it interacts with the chakras, the energy centers that govern various aspects of our physical, emotional, and spiritual well-being. There are seven major chakras aligned along the spine, each corresponding to different levels of consciousness and areas of life.

1. **Muladhara (Root Chakra)**: Located at the base of the spine, this chakra is associated with survival, grounding, and the element of earth. It is the foundation of the physical body and the seat of the dormant kundalini energy.

2. **Svadhisthana (Sacral Chakra)**: Located just below the navel, this chakra is associated with creativity, sexuality, and the element of water. It governs our emotional flow and our connection to pleasure.

3. **Manipura (Solar Plexus Chakra)**: Located at the solar plexus, this chakra is associated with personal power, will, and the element of fire. It is the center of self-esteem and transformation.

4. **Anahata (Heart Chakra)**: Located at the heart, this chakra is associated with love, compassion, and the element of air. It bridges the lower physical chakras and the higher spiritual chakras.

5. **Vishuddha (Throat Chakra)**: Located at the throat, this chakra is associated with communication, truth, and the element of ether. It governs our expression and our ability to speak our truth.

6. **Ajna (Third Eye Chakra)**: Located between the eyebrows, this chakra is associated with intuition, insight, and the element of light. It is the center of perception and inner vision.

7. **Sahasrara (Crown Chakra)**: Located at the top of the head, this chakra is associated with spiritual connection, enlightenment, and the element of thought. It is the gateway to higher consciousness and the divine.

Certain breathwork practices can activate and balance the chakras, allowing the prana to flow freely through them. As each chakra becomes energized, it transforms the corresponding aspects of our lives and elevates our awareness.

❖ EXERCISE: CHAKRA CLEARING MEDITATION

You can perform this practice by having someone read to you aloud, or you can find the recording of this meditation on the Beats and Breath app. You can also use this meditation alongside our "Chakra Breathwork Series," which offers 15-minute sessions through each chakra.

Find a comfortable position, either seated or lying down. Allow your body to relax and your mind to settle. Close your eyes and take a deep breath in, letting it fill your lungs completely. Slowly exhale, releasing any tension or stress. Continue to breathe deeply and evenly, allowing your body to sink into a state of calm.

As you breathe, bring your attention to the base of your spine. This is your Root Chakra, your center of stability and security. Visualize a vibrant red sphere of light glowing warmly at this point. With each breath, imagine this red light expanding, grounding you to the Earth and providing you with strength and stability. Feel a sense of safety and support as this energy becomes more radiant and balanced.

Shift your focus to your lower abdomen, where your Sacral Chakra resides. Envision an orange sphere of light in this area, swirling gently. This is the center of your creativity and emotional well-being. With every inhale, feel this orange light growing brighter and more vibrant. Allow it to enhance your emotional balance and creative energy. Feel a warm, comforting wave of creativity and pleasure flowing through you.

Move your attention upward to your solar plexus, just above your navel. Picture a bright yellow sphere of light glowing in this space. This is your Solar Plexus Chakra, the center of your personal power and confidence. As you breathe in, see this yellow light becoming more intense and powerful. Let it fill you with self-assurance and a sense of purpose. Feel your inner strength and clarity of intention growing with each breath.

Now, focus on your heart center, located in the middle of your chest. Visualize a radiant green sphere of light here, symbolizing love and compassion. As you inhale, imagine this green light expanding outward, filling your entire chest with warmth and kindness. Let this energy embrace you, dissolving any feelings of isolation or sadness. Feel a deep sense of love, forgiveness, and connection with yourself and others.

Next, bring your attention to your throat area, the center of your communication and self-expression. Envision a calming blue sphere of light in this region. With each breath, see this blue light growing clearer and more vibrant. Allow it to enhance your ability to speak your truth and express yourself authentically. Feel your voice becoming stronger and your communication more aligned with your inner self.

Move your focus to the center of your forehead, between your eyebrows. This is your "Third Eye Chakra," the seat of intuition and insight. Visualize a deep indigo sphere of light here, glowing softly. As you breathe in, feel this indigo light growing brighter, opening up your intuitive abilities and inner vision. Allow yourself to connect with your inner wisdom and higher consciousness. Feel clarity and insight flowing into your mind.

Finally, direct your attention to the top of your head, where your Crown Chakra is located. Picture a brilliant violet or white sphere of light at this point, representing spiritual connection and enlightenment. As you breathe deeply, imagine this light expanding, reaching up to the cosmos and connecting you with the universal energy. Feel a sense of unity with the universe and a profound connection to your higher self.

Take a few more deep breaths, allowing all the colors of the chakras to harmonize and flow together in a beautiful, balanced symphony of light. Feel the energy moving smoothly through your entire being, from the base of your spine to the crown of your head.

When you're ready, gently bring your awareness back to the present moment. Wiggle your fingers and toes, and when you feel ready, open your eyes. Carry this balanced and harmonious energy with you throughout your day, knowing that your chakras are aligned and in tune.

THE RISE OF KUNDALINI

In the yogic tradition, Kundalini is often depicted as a coiled serpent resting at the base of the spine. This primal energy represents the divine feminine force, also known as "Shakti," the creative power of the universe. When awakened, Kundalini rises through the body's energy centers, leading to a profound spiritual awakening.

The breath plays a critical role in this process. Pranayama techniques, such as "Bhastrika" (bellows breath) and "Kumbhaka" (breath retention), are specifically designed to stoke the inner fire, gently encouraging the Kundalini energy to uncoil and ascend. As the Kundalini rises, it is said to clear energetic blockages, purify the nadis, and activate the higher chakras, ultimately expanding consciousness.

The awakening of Kundalini is a powerful and transformative experience, often accompanied by intense physical, emotional, and spiritual phenomena. These can include:

- **Energy Movements**: Sensations of energy moving up

the spine, often described as "tingling," "crawling," or "electrical currents."

- **Hot or Cold**: Sudden bursts of heat or cold felt in the body.
- **Shaking or Trembling**: Uncontrollable shaking or trembling, often as the body adjusts to the increased flow of energy.
- **Pressure or Pain**: Sensations of pressure or pain in the head, spine, or other areas, possibly linked to the opening of energy channels.
- **Intense Emotions**: Sudden waves of emotion, from joy and ecstasy to deep sadness, without an apparent cause.
- **Heightened Sensitivity**: Increased sensitivity to emotional and energetic shifts in both oneself and others.
- **Clarity and Insight**: Moments of profound clarity and heightened awareness about life, self, and the universe.
- **Disorientation**: Temporary mental confusion as habitual patterns of thinking are disrupted.
- **Heightened Intuition**: Increased psychic abilities, premonitions, or heightened perceptions.
- **Changes in Interests**: A shift in interests, beliefs, or lifestyle choices that align more closely with spiritual or personal growth.
- **Increased Solitude**: A strong desire for solitude or withdrawal from social interactions as part of processing the awakening.
- **Enhanced Sensitivity**: Greater sensitivity to the energies of people, places, and situations.
- **Healing Experiences**: Spontaneous experiences of physical or emotional healing.

The Kundalini process, while powerful, can be overwhelming if not approached with care. It's essential to practice patience and allow the energy to rise at its own pace, integrating the experiences as they unfold. Should you encounter intense or difficult symptoms, it's important to remain grounded and seek guidance if needed, as this journey unfolds uniquely for each individual.

MY KUNDALINI AWAKENING

Back in 2017, during a time when I had been immersed in the practice of Kundalini yoga, I experienced a profound awakening that altered my perspective and changed the course of my life in many ways. At the time, I could sense that something within me was on the verge of shifting. My devotion to the practice had deepened, and the energy I was stirring through my breath and movement felt potent yet unpredictable.

One night, as I lay in bed, a wave of tremors began to ripple through my body. At first, I thought it was just the residual effects of my practice—muscles relaxing and releasing tension—but soon, the tremors intensified. It felt as though a powerful current of energy was surging through me, rising from the base of my spine with a force I had never experienced before.

My breath quickened as the energy ascended, coursing through every cell. My body shook uncontrollably for nearly three hours while I was caught between two powerful sensations: awe and fear. Fear of the unknown, of the magnitude of what was unfolding within me, and yet awe at the sheer immensity of the experience.

As the tremors coursed through my body, I felt an ancient power awaken within me—terrifying, yet familiar. It was as if my entire nervous system was being rewired, my very being expanded and rearranged in ways that my mind couldn't comprehend at the time. My initial response was to try to understand it, to control it. But then, something miraculous happened—I let go. In that moment of surrender, I stopped resisting and simply allowed the experience to unfold. In the midst of this storm, I felt both fragile and indestructible, small and yet infinitely connected to everything.

And in that surrender, I found peace. A peace so deep and indescribable, it felt as though the universe itself had cracked open within me, revealing hidden layers of wisdom, light, and clarity. The tremors slowly subsided, leaving behind a stillness that was electric, a connection to something far greater than I had ever imagined. It wasn't just energy moving through my body; it was an awakening to a deeper truth, one that redefined how I understood myself and the world around me.

That night marked the beginning of a new journey for me—a journey of expanded consciousness and greater spiritual awakening. I became more attuned to the presence of my soul, feeling its guidance more vividly than ever before. This Kundalini awakening didn't just transform me in that moment; it continues to guide me today, leading me deeper into the mysteries of my own consciousness and the infinite wisdom that lies beyond the mind. It was the first of many steps into the unknown, one that continues to shape my life and my work today.

CEREBROSPINAL FLUID: THE RIVER OF CONSCIOUSNESS

Having undergone multiple awakening experiences, as I've shared in this chapter, I recently began connecting the dots between what was happening on both a biological and metaphysical level. During these profound spiritual moments, I could feel waves of energy coursing through my body—sensations traveling up and down my spine, clearing blockages and expanding my consciousness. For years, I believed these experiences were purely the result of spiritual energy. However, I've come to understand that they are closely tied to the flow of cerebrospinal fluid (CSF).

It was Dr. Mauro Zappaterra's pioneering research that helped me make this connection. A Harvard-trained physician and researcher, Dr. Zappaterra has been at the forefront of studying the relationship between CSF and altered states of consciousness. His work bridges the gap between ancient spiritual traditions and modern science, shedding light on how practices like breathwork influence the body on a deeply biological level.

CSF is a clear, nourishing liquid that bathes the brain and spinal cord, protecting the central nervous system. More than just a protective fluid, CSF plays a vital role in communication within the brain and may be key to accessing higher states of consciousness. Dr. Zappaterra describes CSF as the "fifth circulatory system," placing it alongside blood, lymph, synovial fluid, and interstitial fluid. This elevated my understanding of CSF from a support mechanism to a crucial element in spiritual awakening.

One of the most striking insights from Dr. Zappaterra's research is the idea that CSF not only delivers essential nutrients and signaling molecules but may also act as a conduit for consciousness itself. As it flows through the brain's ventricles and along the spine, CSF helps clear metabolic waste and provides an optimal environment for heightened awareness. The rhythmic movement of CSF—driven by breath, heartbeat, and even subtle spinal movements—creates a harmonic resonance that seems to facilitate expanded consciousness.

This discovery resonated deeply with my own experiences. During my dark room retreat, isolated from external stimuli, I began to feel a deep internal rhythm—like energy flowing up and down my spine with my breath. Looking back, I realize this could have been the flow of CSF, subtly enhanced by the deep, rhythmic breathing and stillness I was practicing. It felt as if this fluid was cleansing me, clearing energetic blockages, and allowing me to access deeper layers of insight and awareness.

Dr. Zappaterra's research also touches on the piezoelectric effect in the brain, where mechanical stress—such as the movement of CSF—creates tiny electrical charges. These charges may influence neural activity, offering an explanation for how breathwork and spinal movements shift states of consciousness. This fascinating convergence of ancient yogic practices and modern neuroscience brings a biological dimension to what yogis have long referred to as the movement of "prana," or life force energy.

One of the most intriguing findings from Dr. Zappaterra's research is the link between breathing patterns and CSF flow. He discovered that deep, rhythmic breathing, particularly in pranayama practices, enhances CSF movement throughout the brain and spine.

This increased flow acts like a "wash cycle" for the brain, clearing away metabolic waste and delivering fresh nutrients that optimize brain function. This cleansing process may create the conditions necessary for expanded states of awareness, something I personally experienced during both my Kundalini awakening and dark room retreat.

Furthermore, the flow of CSF is closely connected to the pineal gland, often referred to as the "third eye" in esoteric traditions. Located in the center of the brain, the pineal gland is sensitive to light, electromagnetic fields, and internal pressure changes caused by breathing practices. It produces melatonin, the hormone that regulates sleep, and is thought to produce DMT (N,N-Dimethyltryptamine), a compound associated with mystical and near-death experiences. By stimulating CSF flow through breath retention techniques and spinal movements, we may be activating the pineal gland, opening the door to heightened spiritual insights, psychic abilities, and inner illumination.

DMT: THE SPIRIT MOLECULE

Often called the "spirit molecule," DMT is known for its ability to induce profound altered states of consciousness. It is produced endogenously, meaning it is created naturally within the human body, and is structurally similar to serotonin and melatonin, two neurotransmitters that play significant roles in the regulation of mood and sleep-wake cycles. Dr. Rick Strassman, a pioneering researcher in this field, proposed that the pineal gland might produce DMT, especially during extraordinary states such as birth, death, and near-death experiences.

DMT is found in Ayahuasca, a traditional South American psychoactive brew mentioned earlier that is primarily used for spiritual and medicinal purposes among indigenous peoples of the Amazon basin. The brew is made from the Banisteriopsis caapi vine and the leaves of the Psychotria viridis shrub, the latter of which supplies the DMT. The vine contains monoamine oxidase inhibitors

(MAOIs), specifically harmala alkaloids, which prevent the breakdown of DMT in the digestive system, thereby allowing it to be active when ingested orally. DMT experiences often share striking similarities with accounts of mystical and spiritual encounters across cultures. Users report sensations of:

1. Transcending time and space
2. Encountering non-physical entities or beings of light
3. Feeling a profound sense of unity with the universe
4. Accessing seemingly infinite realms of knowledge and wisdom

DMT AND THE BREATH: HOW BREATHWORK MIMICS PSYCHEDELIC EXPERIENCES

In the past several years, we have seen the emergence of plant medicines such as psilocybin, iboga, cannabis, peyote, and ayahuasca, as well as psychoactive chemical substances like MDMA, ketamine, and LSD coming into the mainstream scene. Many people, from professional athletes to celebrities to doctors, are speaking about and promoting the use of psychedelics. Historically, many cultures have used plant medicines and psychoactive substances in spiritual and healing practices. Indigenous peoples in various parts of the world, from the Amazon rainforest to the deserts of North America and the faraway lands of India and beyond, have long recognized the therapeutic potential of these substances for physical, mental, emotional and spiritual health.

Although I'm a proponent of psychedelics and have used them myself, it's important to recognize that such journeys into the psyche are not the only path to expanded consciousness. Breathwork stands out as a potent, non-chemical alternative that can also unlock profound states of awareness. It allows us to explore and expand our consciousness without the need for external substances. It enables us to achieve altered states, access deep insights, and experience expanded perceptions through the simple, yet profound, act of controlled breathing.

❖ EXERCISE: HIGHER SELF BREATHWORK JOURNEY

On the Beats and Breath app, we've included a 44-minute breath-work journey titled "Higher Self," which can be found inside the "Master Your Breath, Transform Your Life" compilation. This experience is designed to reconnect you to the wisdom of your soul through a transformative four-round breath practice.

INTEGRATING EXPANDED AWARENESS

As we journey through the cycles of life, we come to realize that each challenge, each moment of discomfort, is a doorway to something greater. The dark nights are not obstacles to be avoided but opportunities for profound growth, essential phases of our evolution. The darkness is not our adversary; it's a sacred space where the old must be shed to make way for the new.

As you walk your own path, remember that growth is not a single event; it's a continuous process. Every breath is an invitation to return to yourself, to peel back the layers of conditioning, and to awaken the light within. The same force that moves through the universe flows within you, and through conscious breathing, you can harness this energy to create, heal, and step into your highest potential.

The journey may not always be easy, but it is always worth it. With each cycle, you draw closer to the truth of your being—more aligned with your purpose, more connected to your soul, and more in tune with the rhythm of life.

Yet, once we've glimpsed the infinite, how do we relate to the finite? After experiencing our oneness with everything, how do we engage with the separateness of everyday existence? In a culture obsessed with chasing peak experiences, the true challenge lies in integrating the wisdom we gain into our daily lives. This is where the real work begins. The Zen saying, "Chop wood, carry water," reminds us that spiritual growth isn't found in constant highs but in performing ordinary tasks with mindfulness and presence. It is in the simplicity of life where deeper lessons become grounded, where insights from moments of clarity and inspiration truly take root.

When Nick and I first began working together in the summer of 2023, he was a struggling musician barely making ends meet. He was filled with self-doubt and couldn't seem to escape the limiting beliefs, negative thought patterns, and insecurities that plagued him in his daily life. He believed he was a victim of life's circumstances and thought the world was out to get him.

In our first few sessions together, I regressed him back to his inner child, where he began to discover the root of his unworthiness. As I guided him into his bodily awareness, he felt an immediate discomfort in his belly—a visceral manifestation of fear. He explained it as a black, suffocating ball of energy that drained his very life force. In his mind's eye, scenes from his childhood flickered like an old film—moments of rejection, shaming, and unmet needs. Tears streamed down his face as he relived the past.

This emotional upheaval was the genesis of Nick's hardened belief system—a relentless inner critic that told him he was unworthy and incapable. This belief system became a prison, confining him to cycles of suffering that bled into every aspect of his life. Financial struggles, creative blocks, vocational frustration, and strained relationships were the tangible results of this internal conflict. To fill the void created by his lack of self-love, Nick fell into the pattern of people-pleasing, placing others' needs above his own in a desperate bid for validation. Yet, this self-sacrifice only deepened the chasm within him, leading to festering resentment and a spiraling cycle of self-doubt and inner turmoil.

Over the following three months, our work together became a transformative journey of healing and renewal. We delved into the depths of his psyche, unraveling old wounds and reframing his beliefs. Each breath was a step toward reprogramming his mindset from one of negativity to one of positive empowerment. As Nick gradually integrated the lost and repressed parts of himself, his inner landscape began to shift. The dark clouds that had long obscured his vision started to part, allowing rays of self-compassion and hope to pierce through.

By the time our sessions drew to a close, Nick's life had undergone a remarkable metamorphosis. He not only found the love of his life, but his music career soared to new heights. His dream house became a tangible reality, a testament to the power of his transformed inner state. Nick's story stands as a powerful testament to the principle that when we align our innermost being—our thoughts, beliefs, perceptions, and energies—with our true desires, we can manifest a life that reflects our deepest aspirations. At the heart of this transformation lies the breath—the sacred rhythm that anchors us in our journey from limitation to limitless possibility.

THE POWER YOU HOLD WITHIN

The concept of manifestation has been spoken about in various ancient texts for many centuries. Yet, in the past two decades, groundbreaking advancements in the realms of quantum physics, quantum mechanics, epigenetics, and beyond have illuminated the profound truth that we possess the intrinsic power to shape our reality. Insights from contemporary pioneers such as Dr. Joe Dispenza, Dr. Bruce Lipton, Dr. Amit Goswami, and Michael B. Beckwith bring new clarity to this ancient understanding, bridging the gap between mystical tradition and modern science.

These visionary thought leaders unraveled the mysteries of how our consciousness interacts with the fabric of reality, revealing that our thoughts, beliefs, and emotions are not mere abstractions; they are potent forces capable of influencing the material world. Their research demonstrates that by harnessing the power of our mind, body, and spirit, we can transcend the realm of wishful thinking and enter a state of profound coherence where our intentions resonate harmoniously with the frequency of our desires.

In the pages ahead, you will embark on a transformative journey to grasp the true essence of manifestation. Drawing from the groundbreaking techniques and teachings of these modern-day trailblazers, you will learn how to align your entire being with your aspirations, using the fundamental tool of your breath to manifest your dreams into reality. This exploration will guide you beyond theoretical concepts into practical applications, empowering you to realize the full potential of your creative power and manifest a life of purpose and fulfillment.

"CONSCIOUS VS. UNCONSCIOUS MANIFESTATION"

At its essence, manifestation is based on a simple yet powerful truth: what you focus on expands. This principle reveals that we are perpetually engaged in the act of manifesting, whether we are doing so consciously or unconsciously.

Our daily lives are often shaped by our trauma. Wounds and societal conditioning instill limiting beliefs, values, and thought patterns, all of which color our perceptions of ourselves and the world around us. This conditioning and programming create a lens through which we view reality, frequently distorting our understanding of what is possible. According to Dr. Joe Dispenza, by the age of 35, we operate on autopilot, with 95 percent of our thoughts, beliefs, and actions driven by unconscious patterns. This autopilot mode reinforces a perception of life happening to us rather than for us, leading us to feel like passive recipients of circumstance rather than active creators of our reality.

In this unconscious state, we often find ourselves ensnared in repetitive cycles of struggle and limitation, perpetuating the same challenges and patterns over and over. Only through conscious awareness and deliberate action can we break free from these cycles. By taking full ownership of our healing journey and reclaiming our power, we awaken to our true, authentic selves and step into our role as conscious creators.

Conscious manifestation is, therefore, the intentional practice of aligning your thoughts, beliefs, emotions, energy, and actions with your desires, dreams, and goals. It is a process of transforming internal visions into external realities. This practice demands a profound level of presence, trust, and surrender. To manifest consciously, you must cultivate a deep connection with your inner self, allowing your heart-based intentions to guide your actions while maintaining a harmonious balance between desire and acceptance, knowing that you are also co-creating with a higher intelligence.

At its core, conscious manifestation is about recognizing and harnessing the inherent power within you to shape your experiences. It is an ongoing dance between envisioning your ideal outcomes and taking purposeful steps to bring them into being. It is not just about intellectual understanding; it is about embodiment. It is an invitation to become the conscious creator of your own life, using the breath as a sacred tool to breathe life into your vision and bridge the gap between your inner world and the reality you wish to experience. So it may be worth asking yourself: What masterpiece do you want to create?

THE SCIENCE AND SPIRIT OF CREATION

Dr. Joe Dispenza often says, "Your personality creates your personal reality." But what if we could consciously choose our personality—and thus our reality—with each breath we take? This is not mere wishful thinking; it is a profound truth supported by the latest findings in neuroscience, epigenetics, and quantum physics.

At the core of Dr. Dispenza's work is the concept of neuroplasticity—the brain's ability to reorganize itself by forming new neural connections. Every thought we think and every emotion we feel triggers a cascade of neurochemical reactions, strengthening certain neural pathways while weakening others. This process quite literally reshapes our brain.

When we engage in focused breathwork combined with visualization and elevated emotions, we create a powerful cocktail for neural change. The regulated breathing calms the autonomic nervous system, reducing stress hormones like cortisol and increasing feel-good neurotransmitters like serotonin and dopamine, allowing us to enter a state of relaxation and presence in which we can align our imagination with our desired outcome (more on this later).

As Dr. Dispenza explains in his book "Breaking the Habit of Being Yourself", when we repeatedly practice thinking and feeling in new ways, we build new neural networks. Over time, these new patterns of thinking and feeling become our default state—effectively changing our personality and, by extension, our personal reality.

EPIGENETICS: THE BIOLOGY OF BELIEF

At the cellular level, pioneering biologist Dr. Bruce Lipton has shown that our beliefs and perceptions shape our biological reality. His research in epigenetics reveals that our thoughts and emotions can actually turn genes on or off, influencing our physical and mental states.

Lipton's work, detailed in The Biology of Belief, demonstrates that the cell membrane—not the nucleus—is the brain of the cell. This membrane contains receptors that respond to environmental signals, including the chemistry of our thoughts and emotions. When we change our perceptions (through practices like mindful breathing and visualization), we change the signals sent to our cells, potentially altering gene expression.

This means that, through conscious breathing and intentional thought, we can influence our biology at the most fundamental level. We're not merely victims of our genetic inheritance but active participants in our biological destiny.

QUANTUM PHYSICS AND CONSCIOUSNESS

The field of quantum physics offers perhaps the most mind-bending support for the power of conscious creation. Unlike the predictable world of classical physics, the quantum realm is one of probabilities and potentials.

Dr. Amit Goswami, theoretical quantum physicist and author of The Self-Aware Universe, proposes that consciousness, not matter, is the fundamental reality of the universe. In this view, our conscious observations and intentions can influence the collapse of quantum possibilities into concrete realities.

This aligns with the famous double-slit experiment, which shows that the mere act of observation can change the behavior of particles at the quantum level. When we extrapolate this to our daily lives, it suggests that our innermost state of consciousness—our intention and belief—directly influences our external reality.

Spiritual teacher and founder of the Agape International Spiritual Center, Dr. Michael Beckwith, shares his four stages of evolutionary growth in his book Life Visioningthat serve as a template or roadmap to help you shift from unconscious to conscious creator. The four stages include:

1. **Victim Consciousness:** This state of consciousness is characterized by a belief that one is a victim of circumstances and has little control over one's life. Individuals in victim consciousness often feel powerless and blame others for their problems.

2. **Manifester Consciousness:** This state of consciousness is characterized by a belief that one has the power to create one's reality through positive thinking and intention. Individuals in manifester consciousness are proactive in creating the life they desire.

3. **Channeler Consciousness:** This state of consciousness is characterized by a belief that one is a channel for divine inspiration and guidance. Individuals in channeler consciousness seek to align themselves with the wisdom and guidance of the Divine to live a purposeful life.

4. **Being Consciousness:** This state of consciousness is characterized by a sense of unity and interconnectedness with all of creation. Individuals in Being consciousness are able to transcend ego-driven concerns and experience a deeper sense of peace and fulfillment.

THE HEART-BRAIN CONNECTION

The HeartMath Institute conducts fascinating research on the connection between the heart and brain and how this relates to our ability to manifest our desires. They've found that the heart generates a powerful electromagnetic field that can be measured several feet away from the body.

When we enter a state of "coherence our heart rhythm, breathing, and brain waves are synchronized—this field becomes even stronger and more organized. This coherent state is associated with improved cognitive function, intuition, and even an increased ability to "attract" and "magnetize" positive experiences.

Conscious breathing is one of the fastest ways to induce this coherent state. By practicing heart-focused breathing (imagining breathing through your heart), you can quickly shift into a state of psychophysiological coherence, enhancing your capacity for clear thinking and intentional creation.

THE POWER OF THE WORD

"And God said, 'Let there be light,' and there was light." Genesis 1:3

Words are powerful tools of creation. The language we use influences how we perceive ourselves and create the world around us. In essence, words are self-fulfilling prophecies, carrying magnetic and potent energy that can either build up or tear down. If you constantly tell yourself, "I am unlucky," you will subconsciously sabotage opportunities, confirming your belief. Conversely, saying "Good things happen to me" can open your mind to noticing and acting on positive opportunities, thus manifesting higher outcomes. Therefore, when we speak positively about our desires and goals, we align ourselves with those outcomes, helping to bring them into our reality.

When we speak positively about our desires and goals, we align ourselves with those outcomes, helping to bring them into our reality. Allow your language to become a tool that serves you, not harms you.

CHANGE YOUR STATE. CHANGE YOUR LIFE

When we synthesize these various fields of study—neuroscience, epigenetics, consciousness, and heart coherence research—we begin to see a comprehensive framework for creation. Our breath serves as the bridge between these realms. As we breathe, we are literally shifting our energy and vibrational state. By speaking and then breathing in our intention, we're not just exchanging oxygen and carbon dioxide— we're participating in a profound dance of creation at the quantum, cellular, and neurological levels that ultimately help us enter coherent states, access altered consciousness, and embody new emotional states, drawing in the infinite possibilities of the quantum field.

Having worked with hundreds of people over the years, I have created actionable and powerful blueprints in the form of tools and exercises to help people heal their past, discover their purpose, and close the gap between where they are and where they want to be. Therefore, below you'll find several very powerful practices, prompts, and exercises to magnetize greater abundance and manifest your dream reality.

❖ EXERCISE: "MAGNETIZING AND MANIFESTING YOUR DREAM REALITY"

This is a five-step process I have used on myself and many others. For the first four steps of this exercise, I recommend finding a quiet space, setting aside one hour, and recording your answers to each question on a notepad, in a journal, or on the computer. After you've done so, you can go to the "Beats and Breath" app for a guided manifestation breathwork journey.

Step 1: Uncover Your Core Values: Your core values are your fundamental driving forces. These are your true priorities that often get buried under what society—i.e., your community, family, friends, etc.—tells you to be, love, and do. You may have a long list of values off the top of your head, but your core values are deeply ingrained within your being. They are often difficult to detect with your conscious awareness until you do the work to reveal them. Whether you're aware of these values or not, they are your inner compass, guiding you to the fullest expression of your truest self. Many of us lose touch with our core values because we spend our entire lives living according to societal standards and expectations. This can lead to fleeting happiness, confusion, difficult decision-making, feeling that something is "missing" in your life, and an overall lack of fulfillment.

The intention of this exercise is to help you get clear on what's most important to you on a soul-based level ("soul" meaning your unique individuality and the expression of that individuality through your natural gifts, talents, and skills). Once you've identified your core values, you have an opportunity to align all areas of your life, such as your relationships, passions, and career, with your values.

Before identifying your six to eight core values, answer the questions below:

a. When you were at your happiest in life, what were you doing? Who were you with? Where did you live?
b. When was a time you felt passionate about your life or work? Describe this time in detail.
c. What were the greatest lessons you learned from adversity?
d. Observe the times when you were particularly upset or angry. What was missing for you?
e. Think of a fulfilling day you've had recently at work. What about this day was enjoyable?

Take a look at the list of common values on this page. Circle, highlight, or write down on a separate sheet of paper the top six to eight that are important to your overall well-being. Remember to choose what you believe your values already are, and not what you want them to be! It is very important to be honest with yourself about what you presently value instead of claiming values you wish you had or values you feel you are expected to have.

You may find some of the values naturally combine. For instance, if you value service, community, and generosity, you may combine them into "helping others." If necessary, you can create your own title for a value that encompasses many other values on the list.

Accountability
Adventure
Ambition
Authenticity
Authority
Autonomy
Balance
Beauty
Belonging
Boldness

Calmness
Commitment
Community
Compassion
Consistency
Contribution
Cooperation
Courtesy
Creativity
Curiosity
Decisiveness
Dedication
Dependability
Determination
Diplomacy
Discipline
Discretion
Diversity
Dynamism
Efficiency
Elegance
Empathy
Equality
Excellence
Exploration
Faith
Family
Freedom
Friendship
Generosity
Grace
Growth
Happiness
Harmony
Health

Helping others
Honesty
Humility
Humor
Independence
Influence
Ingenuity
Intelligence
Intuition
Joy
Justice
Kindness
Knowledge
Leadership
Learning
Legacy
Love
Loyalty
Mastery
Openness
Optimism
Originality
Peace
Positivity
Purpose
Practicality
Prosperity
Recognition
Reliability
Religion
Resourcefulness
Respect
Responsibility
Security
Self-actualization

Sensitivity
Simplicity
Spirituality
Spontaneity
Stability
Status
Strategy
Structure
Success
Support
Teamwork
Temperance
Thankfulness
Thoroughness
Thoughtfulness
Trust
Uniqueness
Unity
Wisdom

Follow-Up Questions

a. Are you proud of your core values?
b. Do these values represent things you would support, even if your choice isn't popular with the mainstream?
c. Do you feel good about yourself when you read your values?
d. List the values you chose and on a scale of 1 to 10, rate how much you are presently honoring that value in your life.
e. When is a time you honored each value fully? What was the experience? How did it feel?
f. What is one barrier or obstacle that keeps you from fully honoring each value now?

g. What can you do to start overcoming these barriers?

Step 2: Identify Your Passions: Excitement is one of the most powerful precursors to experiencing greater fulfillment, prosperity, and success. When you follow your excitement (without expectation or attachment), you live in the flow with life. Within this excitement is a core ingredient: passion. Your passions don't necessarily need to translate to your daily vocation or your work, but they do offer a clear signal as to where your excitement lies. Therefore, by implementing them into your life, you will naturally experience more satisfaction, creativity, and overall well-being. Unfortunately, most of us have lost our zest and excitement for life along the way. The questions below are designed to help you reconnect with the wondrous, imaginative, and curious soul you once were, allowing you to rekindle the flame so you can begin living a passion-filled life.

a. When you were a child, what activities brought you the most joy?

b. When have you been so absorbed in something that you lost track of time? What were you doing?

c. If you were accidentally locked in a bookshop overnight, which section(s) would you camp out in?

d. What topic could you give a 30-minute presentation that would light you up?

e. Which of your needs and values are being sacrificed by ignoring your passions?

f. What inspires you at this point in your life?

g. What roadblocks are in the way of enjoying your passions presently?

h. How can you begin to prioritize your time to ensure plenty of time to explore these passions?

i. In what ways are you willing to experiment with implementing your passions into your daily life?

j. How can your passions help others?

Step 3: Clarify Your Vision: Your vision is the first step towards creating the life you desire; one in which you are living in the full embodiment of your creative genius, unique gifts and higher purpose. Visioning provides awareness and sets the stage for action, establishing the blueprint for bringing your intentions, desires and dreams into reality. By nurturing and holding your highest vision in your field, you gain direction on your path and align with the necessary people and experiences to bring this vision to life. Having a clear vision doesn't mean your life will be void of challenges. In fact, when we begin to pursue this vision, we will be met with obstacles that will test our faith and patience. It's your own inner transformation, and the way in which you adapt to these challenges is what brings this vision to life. Remember, nothing is off limits. Imagine you have a magic wand. What ideal future would you create for yourself? Allow your thoughts and imagination to run wild. Consider each of the foundational areas of your life when answering the questions: Career, Financial, Social, Family, Relationships, Health, Spiritual, Etc.

1. If money weren't an issue and you could do anything, what would it be? Step into a realm of limitless possibility. What experiences do you desire to have in your ultimate dream life? What's on your bucket list? Some examples may include becoming a bestselling author, a motivational speaker at TEDx, and so on. Allow your imagination to run wild. After you've written them down, use the power of your words and speak them out. Review this list every day for at least thirty days.

2. For these experiences to come to life, in what areas would you need to grow and transform? What limiting beliefs or thought-forms do you need to let go? What negative behaviors or patterns do you need to release? What new skills and abilities do you need to strengthen?

a. Imagine a eulogy honoring your life contribution and accomplishments. How have you made an impact in the lives of others? List all the ways you would make a difference in the world.

b. (Optional) Complete the 'Vision Quest' breathwork session on the Beats and Breath app.

<u>Step 4: Harness the Power of Gratitude:</u> Gratitude is the oxygen to our soul. It is the frequency that aligns us with goodness and beauty. It is the fuel that propels us into a life of abundance, happiness, and freedom. When you connect with the essence of gratitude, you create a positive physiological and psychological response that shifts the way you feel within yourself and the world around you.

a. Create a list of 100 things you're grateful for. This is designed to stretch your imagination so you consider every area of your life in which you have something to appreciate and be thankful for.

b. Circle the ones that create a visceral reaction in your body.

c. Sit with those sensations and allow gratitude to fill your body.

d. (Optional) Complete the 'Gratitude' breathwork session on the Beats and Breath app.

<u>Step 5: Breathe Your Way To Bliss:</u> We've created a revolutionary and highly impactful breathwork journey titled "Manifest" on the Beats and Breath app. This journey is specifically designed to open your energetic channels, raise your vibrational energy, and connect you to your highest vision. When in this heightened state of presence, you are able to tap into the limitless realm of possibilities to create significant change inside and out. For maximum results, I recommend doing this practice each day for 30 days.

TRUST, SURRENDER, ALLOW

After taking intentional action through the exercises we've explored, there comes a crucial next step: trust, surrender, and allow. While manifestation is powered by our ability to envision and act, it also requires that we release control and trust in the universe to guide the process. The balance between inspired action and letting go is where the true magic of manifestation unfolds.

Trust is knowing that the energy you've put out into the world will return to you in the form of your desires. It's the deep belief that once you've set your intentions and taken meaningful steps toward your goals, the universe and your higher self will take care of the rest. Trust invites you to release any doubt or fear, knowing that even if the outcome doesn't unfold exactly as you expect, it will be what's most aligned with your highest good. Trust creates space for the universe to support you, allowing synchronicities and opportunities to flow your way, often in surprising forms.

Once you've placed your trust in the process, it's essential to surrender. Surrendering is not about giving up; it's about releasing your attachment to specific outcomes and rigid timelines. You've done the inner and outer work; now it's time to let go of the need to control every detail. Surrendering allows you to step back and invite in the guidance of your higher self, trusting that the universe may have a better path in mind than what your limited view can see. When you surrender, you're acknowledging that manifestation isn't just about forcefully making things happen, but about allowing life to flow through you in alignment with your desires.

Lastly, you must allow. Allowing means giving yourself permission to receive what you've asked for. So often, we block our own manifestations by staying in a state of doubt or by clinging too tightly to how we think things should happen. To allow is to open up energetically, to release resistance, and to let the universe deliver in ways that might surprise or surpass your expectations. It's about making peace with the process and trusting that what's coming your way is exactly what you need, even if it looks different from what you originally envisioned.

This trifecta of trust, surrender, and allowing is what transforms manifestation from a mental exercise into a co-creative dance with the universe. You've taken the aligned actions; now it's time to step back, trust in the unseen forces at work, surrender the need for control, and allow the universe to deliver.

Remember, manifestation isn't just about making things happen —it's about letting things happen. When you align your energy with your desires and allow the universe to play its part, you create the conditions for miracles. This balance of action and release is what allows your dreams to take shape, often in ways far more beautiful than you could have imagined.

THE BREATH OF CREATION

As you've seen throughout this chapter, the power to manifest your dreams lies not in some far-off mystical realm but within you. By aligning your mind, body, and spirit with your deepest desires and allowing the journey to unfold according to divine will, you become the conscious creator of your life rather than a passive observer. The breath is the gateway to this power—the bridge between your inner world of intention and the outer world of reality. Each inhale invites clarity, and each exhale releases doubt. With every breath, you are actively shaping your future.

In mastering the breath, you master the art of conscious creation. You have the tools within you to transform your reality—to heal your past, to craft a future filled with purpose, abundance, and joy. The journey of manifestation is ongoing, and as you continue to breathe life into your vision, remember that you hold the power within. Trust in your power, live in the process, and watch as the dreams unfold before your eyes.

MASTERING YOUR BREATHWORK PRACTICE

Like a garden that needs tending, your breathwork practice requires care, intention, and devotion. My greatest intention is to guide you in cultivating a practice that will flourish and grow, nourishing your body, mind, and spirit. As you learned in the previous chapters, the benefits of breathwork are profound, but the key to unlocking these benefits lies in establishing and maintaining a consistent practice. In this chapter, you will learn how to build a sacred space for your practice, set meaningful intentions, and integrate breathwork into your daily routine.

As you nurture this practice, it will become a source of strength and serenity—a place you can return to again and again for renewal and inspiration. Each breath you take within your practice is a seed planted in the soil of your soul, promising a harvest of transformation and growth.

ESTABLISHING A REGULAR PRACTICE

Creating a regular breathwork practice is essential for reaping the full benefits. Here are some tips to get started:

- **Set Clear Goals**: Determine what you want to achieve with your breathwork practice. Whether it's stress reduction, improved focus, or emotional healing, having clear goals will help you stay motivated and track your progress.
- **Choose a Convenient Time**: Select a time of day that fits seamlessly into your schedule. For some, early mornings are ideal for setting a positive tone for the day, while others may find evening sessions helpful for winding down. You can go to the settings of the Beats and Breath app and choose which days and times work best for you, and the app will send you reminders.
- **Create a Dedicated Space**: Designate a specific area in your home for breathwork. This space should be quiet, comfortable, and free from distractions. Personalize it with items that promote relaxation, such as an eye mask, candles, essential oils, and crystals.
- **Start Small**: Begin with short, manageable sessions. Even 5 to 10 minutes a day can be effective. Gradually increase the duration as you become more comfortable with the practice. We offer various session lengths on our app, ranging from 5 to 45 minutes.
- **Consistency is Key**: Aim to practice daily. Consistency helps build a habit and allows you to experience the cumulative benefits of breathwork. Use reminders or set a routine to reinforce your commitment.
- **Track Your Progress**: Keep a journal or use our app to record your breathwork sessions, noting any changes in mood, energy levels, or overall well-being. This will help you stay motivated and identify patterns in your practice.

CREATING DAILY RITUALS TO STAY CONNECTED

These rituals don't need to be time-consuming; they simply need to be intentional, offering you moments throughout your day to pause, reflect, and reconnect.

1. **Morning Breath Ritual: Setting the Tone for Your Day**
   - Start each day with a simple breathwork practice to set the tone for what's ahead. Upon waking, sit up in bed, close your eyes, and take five slow, deep breaths. As you inhale, set an intention for the day, such as "I choose peace," "I embrace joy," or "I am open to possibilities." This ritual helps you begin your day with clarity, focus, and a sense of purpose. You can also set a daily reminder on the Beats and Breath app to notify you when it's time to practice.
2. **Midday Check-In: Breathing Space**
   - Amidst the busyness of your day, take a few minutes to check in with yourself. Pause whatever you're doing, close your eyes, and take three conscious breaths. Notice how you're feeling physically, emotionally, and mentally. This quick reset allows you to reconnect with yourself and adjust your energy as needed.
3. **Evening Reflection: Letting Go of the Day**
   - Before bed, spend a few moments with your breath to release the events of the day. Sit quietly, close your eyes, and inhale deeply through your nose, holding for a moment at the top. As you exhale, imagine releasing any stress, tension, or lingering thoughts. Use this time to express gratitude for the day's experiences, both the good and the challenging.

CUSTOMIZING YOUR BREATHWORK PRACTICE

Tailoring your breathwork practice to fit your lifestyle, needs, and goals will enhance its effectiveness. Consider these strategies for customization:

- **Understand Your Needs**: Reflect on what you need most from your practice. Are you looking for stress relief, emotional balance, or increased energy? Choose techniques that align with these needs. Our growing breathwork library offers various intentions and themes.
- **Integrate Breathwork into Daily Life**: Bring conscious breathing into your daily activities, such as your morning routine, during your commute, or as a break during work. Integrating breathwork into your life doesn't require grand gestures; it's about creating small, meaningful rituals that bring you back to your center, transforming ordinary moments into sacred pauses.
- **Adjust for Lifestyle Changes**: As your life evolves, your breathwork practice may need to adapt. Be flexible and willing to adjust your practice to fit new circumstances, such as changes in work schedules or personal responsibilities.
- **Seek Professional Guidance**: If you have specific goals or challenges, consider working with a "Beats and Breath" breathwork coach or instructor who can provide personalized guidance and help you refine your practice.

OVERCOMING CHALLENGES IN BREATHWORK

Maintaining a breathwork practice is not without its challenges. Here's how to overcome common obstacles:

- **Resistance and Doubt**: It's normal to experience resistance or doubt, especially when starting something new. Remind yourself of the benefits and be patient. Keep a positive mindset and trust the process.

- **Inconsistency**: Life can be unpredictable, and maintaining consistency can be tough. Develop a routine that fits your lifestyle and use reminders or cues to stay on track. If you miss a session, don't be discouraged—simply resume your practice as soon as possible.
- **Lack of Motivation**: To stay motivated, set small, achievable milestones and celebrate your progress. Joining a breathwork group or community can also provide support and accountability.
- **Physical Discomfort**: If you experience physical discomfort, adjust your technique or consult with a professional to ensure you're practicing correctly. Comfort is important for a sustainable practice.
- **Emotional Resistance**: Breathwork can bring up intense emotions. Acknowledge these feelings and approach them with curiosity and compassion. Remember, this is part of the healing process.

INTEGRATING BREATHWORK INTO DAILY LIFE

Breathwork is not just a practice; it's a tool that can enhance various aspects of your life. Here's how to integrate breathwork into your daily routine:

- **At Work**: Use breathwork techniques to manage stress and increase focus. Simple exercises like deep breathing or box breathing can be done at your desk or during breaks, helping to maintain calm and clarity throughout the workday.
- **In Relationships**: Apply breathwork to enhance communication and emotional connection. Practicing deep breathing before or during difficult conversations

can help you stay centered and responsive rather than reactive.

- **During Self-Care**: Combine breathwork with other self-care practices such as meditation, yoga, or journaling. This integration creates a holistic approach to well-being and deepens your self-care routine.
- **In Crisis Situations**: Use breathwork to manage acute stress or anxiety. Simple, calming techniques can provide immediate relief and help you regain composure during challenging moments.
- **For Long-Term Benefits**: Consistent breathwork practice supports overall health and well-being. It can improve sleep quality, enhance emotional resilience, boost creativity, and promote a sense of inner peace.

STORIES OF TRANSFORMATION

Each day, I am reminded why I do what I do, drawing inspiration from the countless individuals who have transformed their lives through breathwork. Here are five short stories of transformation from Sonic Breathwork™ participants around the world:

1. **Emma's Story – Overcoming Anxiety**
   - Emma, a busy mother of three, found herself constantly overwhelmed by anxiety, often feeling on the verge of panic. After incorporating just 10 minutes of breathwork into her morning routine, Emma began to notice significant changes. Her anxiety levels decreased and she felt more present and connected with her family. Breathwork became her sanctuary, providing her with a much-needed pause in the chaos of daily life.
2. **David's Story – Rediscovering Creativity**
   - David, a graphic designer, felt creatively blocked for months. His work, which he once loved, had become a

source of frustration. A friend recommended breathwork, and within weeks, David felt a shift. He described his sessions as a "gateway back to inspiration," allowing ideas to flow freely once more. Breathwork reconnected him to his creative spark and renewed his passion for his craft.

3. **Sophia's Story – Healing from Grief**
   - After losing her father, Sophia was drowning in grief and struggling to find a way forward. She felt stuck in her pain, unable to move on. Through breathwork, Sophia was able to process her emotions in a safe and supportive way. She began to release the heaviness in her heart, finding solace and healing with each breath. Breathwork became a gentle guide through her journey of loss, helping her find peace amid her sorrow.

4. **Carlos's Story – Managing Chronic Pain**
   - Carlos, who suffered from chronic back pain, was skeptical that breathwork could help him. But after trying a session focused on pain relief and relaxation, he was amazed by the results. The breathwork helped him manage his pain levels, reducing his reliance on medication. Carlos found that breathwork not only eased his physical discomfort, it improved his overall quality of life, allowing him to engage more fully in daily activities.

5. **Jenna's Story – Building Confidence**
   - Jenna struggled with self-doubt and a lack of confidence, especially in social situations. She often felt disconnected from herself and unsure of her place in the world. Breathwork helped her quiet the negative self-talk and reconnect with her inner strength. Over time, Jenna noticed a shift—she felt more grounded, empowered, and capable of showing

up authentically. Breathwork became a daily reminder of her inherent worth and potential.

6. **Steven's Story – Battling Burnout**
   - Steven, a high-achieving corporate executive, was burning the candle at both ends. He was constantly stressed, exhausted, and on the brink of burnout. Despite his success, Steven felt disconnected from his purpose and overwhelmed by the demands of his job. He started practicing breathwork during his lunch breaks as a way to reset and recharge. Within weeks, he noticed a profound shift in his energy and mindset. Breathwork became his lifeline—a tool to manage stress and reconnect with his inner calm. As Steven continued his practice, he gained clarity on his priorities, setting healthier boundaries and rediscovering a sense of balance that had long been missing from his life.

Breathwork is not a one-time solution; it's a lifelong journey that grows with you, evolves as you do, and supports you through every stage of your life. Each breath is an invitation to explore deeper levels of awareness, connection, and presence, offering new insights and experiences along the way. As you continue to deepen your breathwork practice, you may find yourself drawn to new techniques, communities, and opportunities that further enrich your journey. Whether through advanced practices, spiritual exploration, joining a breathwork group, or becoming a practitioner, the path of breathwork is limitless—expanding your understanding of yourself and the world around you. If you want to learn more about our "Beats and Breath Certified Training Program," you can visit the additional resources section in the back of the book.

LIVING A BREATH-CENTERED LIFE

As you stand on the threshold of a new reality, having explored the depths of breathwork and its profound impact on your mind, body, and spirit, one essential question remains: How do you take the knowledge, practices, and insights you've gained and weave them into the fabric of your daily life? How do you create a life that is not only more fulfilling and meaningful but also deeply connected, authentic, and aligned with your true self?

Living a breath-centered life means infusing every moment with the awareness and grace that your breath offers. It's about being fully alive—appreciating the beauty and simplicity of the present—and embracing with an open heart whatever life brings. The breath becomes your ultimate guide and companion: a source of calm amidst the chaos, a catalyst for growth, and a tool for grounding yourself in the here and now. Beyond your personal connection to the breath, you can use it to enhance every aspect of your life—from relationships to business, to parenting, and beyond.

BREATH-CENTERED RELATIONSHIPS

As you deepen your relationship with your breath, it naturally extends to your connections with others. A breath-centered life fosters greater empathy, patience, and understanding—qualities essential for healthy and fulfilling relationships. In moments of conflict or tension, the breath serves as an anchor, allowing you to ground yourself and listen more deeply. Instead of reacting impulsively, you can pause, take a deep breath, and respond with clarity and compassion.

Consider practicing breathwork with your loved ones as a way to connect on a deeper, more intimate level. This can be as simple as sitting together in silence, breathing in unison, or engaging in a guided breathwork session as a couple or family. Synchronizing your breath creates a sense of harmony and shared presence, enhancing communication and building trust. It transforms shared moments into sacred experiences, deepening intimacy and creating a safe space where everyone feels seen, heard, and valued.

In relationships, the breath can also be used as a powerful tool for healing. By breathing together through moments of pain or misunderstanding, you create an environment where emotions can be processed and released, rather than suppressed or projected. This shared breathwork practice strengthens bonds and cultivates a deeper sense of safety, security, and connection with those you care about most.

BREATH-CENTERED BUSINESS

Breathwork isn't just for personal growth—it can revolutionize the way we work and lead. Bringing breath into the workplace, whether you're a solopreneur, team leader, or company founder, can significantly boost productivity, enhance creativity, improve decision-making, and foster a culture of well-being. In my work with executives and leaders across various organizations, I've seen firsthand how integrating breathwork can elevate not just individual performance but also the collective energy of a team.

For instance, starting meetings with a few minutes of mindful breathing can set a calm and collaborative tone, reducing stress and enhancing clarity. Breathwork is also a powerful tool for managing high-pressure situations, helping leaders remain grounded and make thoughtful, strategic decisions—even in the face of challenges.

Encouraging breathwork in the workplace promotes a culture that values mental and emotional health, leading to increased employee retention, job satisfaction, and overall productivity. Breath-centered business practices remind us that success is not just about output and performance; it's about creating an environment where individuals feel empowered, supported, and connected to a greater vision and purpose. If you want to dive deeper into how you can support yourself and your teams, be sure to check out Beats and Breath Corporate Breathwork offerings found in additional resources.

BREATH-CENTERED PARENTING AND FAMILY LIFE

One of the greatest gifts you can give your children is the power of breath. Children are naturally attuned to their breath, often breathing deeply and fully without the constraints of stress or anxiety. However, as they grow and experience the pressures of life, their breath patterns can shift, reflecting their inner emotional states.

Teaching your children about breathwork equips them with a lifelong tool for self-regulation, emotional resilience, and inner peace. I remember when my son was just two years old; I placed a pair of headphones over his ears and played one of our short "Beats and Breath" sessions. Instinctively, he began synchronizing his breath with the beat of the music. Since then, we've incorporated breathwork into our daily routine, practicing together in the morning, throughout the day, and before bedtime to help him manage his emotions and find a sense of calm.

Children can benefit immensely from breathwork, learning to use their breath to navigate big emotions like fear, frustration, and sadness. Whether it's through playful breath games or guided sessions, breathwork can become a bonding activity that fosters connection, mindfulness, and emotional intelligence. Our "Beats and Breath" app includes a dedicated children's section, offering guided breathwork sessions tailored specifically for young ones, helping them cultivate inner calm and focus.

BREATH-CENTERED LIVING: BEYOND THE PERSONAL

Breathwork extends far beyond personal, business, or family life—it's a practice that connects us to something greater. As you move forward, let your breath be a constant reminder of your connection to the vast, intelligent universe that supports, guides, and responds to your intentions. Living a breath-centered life means aligning with this universal flow and stepping into greater freedom, authenticity, and joy.

- **In Moments of Stress or Crisis**: Breathwork can be your first line of defense. Simple practices like deep diaphragmatic breathing or box breathing can quickly calm your nervous system and help you navigate challenging situations with grace and poise.
- **As a Tool for Personal Growth**: Use breathwork to break through personal limitations, tap into your inner wisdom, and access new levels of creativity and insight. Breath-centered living is about constantly evolving, growing, and expanding your consciousness.
- **As a Daily Ritual**: Infuse breathwork into your morning routine, your commute, your workout, or your evening wind-down. These small, intentional moments of breath can transform mundane tasks into sacred rituals that center and ground you throughout the day.
- **As a Path to Spiritual Connection**: For those seeking deeper spiritual growth, breathwork can be a gateway to

profound states of awareness and connection with the divine. It's a way to quiet the mind, open the heart, and experience the peace and presence that lie beyond the thinking mind.

As you continue this journey, know that your breath is not just a tool for managing stress or navigating daily challenges—it's a sacred guide, an ever-present reminder of your own capacity to create, heal, and transform. With every conscious breath, you are building a bridge to a more empowered, intentional life, aligning with the limitless possibilities that await.

Living a breath-centered life means embodying presence, purpose, and possibility in each moment. As you step forward from this chapter, trust that your breath will always lead you back to your center, reminding you of your strength, your wisdom, and your capacity to live fully.

May your path be illuminated with joy, abundance, and clarity. Breathe deeply, live boldly, and let your breath be the compass that guides you to your most authentic, liberated self. Peace.

ADDITIONAL RESOURCES

To deepen your journey and fully experience the transformative power of breathwork, below you'll find additional resources to support you beyond the pages of this book.

Download the Beats and Breath App
Apple iOS

Download the Beats and Breath App Google Android

Beats and Breath App
https://beatsandbreath.com
Beats and Breath Facilitator Program
https://beatsandbreath.com/facilitator
Beats and Breath Corporate
 https://beatsandbreath.com/corporate/
Become a Sonic Breathwork™ Facilitator
Beats and Breath Certified Facilitator Program
Coaching
https://www.christopheraugust.co/coaching
Corporate Breathwork
Beats and Breath Corporate Program
1-1 Coaching with Christopher
SoulSource™ Session
VIP Mastery Coaching
SoulSource Session
 https://www.christopheraugust.co/soulsource

BIBLIOGRAPHY

Beckwith, Michael. Life Visioning: A Transformative Process for Activating Your Unique Gifts and Highest Potential. Sounds True, 2011.

Dispenza, Joe. Breaking the Habit of Being Yourself: How to Lose Your Mind and Create a New One. Hay House, 2012.

Dispenza, Joe. Becoming Supernatural: How Common People Are Doing the Uncommon. Hay House, 2017.

Goswami, Amit. The Self-Aware Universe: How Consciousness Creates the Material World. TarcherPerigee, 1995.

Grof, Stanislav, and Christina Grof. Holotropic Breathwork: A New Approach to Self-Exploration and Therapy. SUNY Press, 2010.

Jung, Carl. The Archetypes and the Collective Unconscious. Princeton University Press, 1959.

Levine, Peter. Waking the Tiger: Healing Trauma. North Atlantic Books, 1997.

Lipton, Bruce. The Biology of Belief: Unleashing the Power of Consciousness, Matter & Miracles. Hay House, 2005.

Maté, Gabor. When the Body Says No: The Cost of Hidden Stress. Knopf Canada, 2003.

Maté, Gabor. The Myth of Normal: Trauma, Illness, and Healing in a Toxic Culture. Avery, 2022.

Nestor, James. Breath: The New Science of a Lost Art. Riverhead Books, 2020.

Orr, Leonard, and Sondra Ray. Rebirthing in the New Age. Celestial Arts, 1977.

Rudd, Richard. The Gene Keys: Unlocking the Higher Purpose Hidden in Your DNA. Watkins Publishing, 2013.

Strassman, Rick.DMT: The Spirit Molecule. Park Street Press, 2000.

Zappaterra, Mauro. Consciousness and Cerebrospinal Fluid Flow. Unpublished research papers and lectures.